HE SAW *Himself* IN ALL *His* CREATURES

A MOTHER'S REMEMBRANCE

HE SAW *Himself*
IN ALL *His* CREATURES

A MOTHER'S REMEMBRANCE

HELEN NORRIE

GREAT PLAINS
PUBLICATIONS

Great Plains Publications
420 – 70 Arthur Street
Winnipeg, MB R3B 1G7
www.greatplains.mb.ca

Great Plains Publications gratefully acknowledges the financial
support provided for its publishing program by the Government
of Canada through the Book Publishing Industry Development
Program (BPIDP); the Canada Council for the Arts; as well as the
Manitoba Department of Culture, Heritage and Tourism; and the
Manitoba Arts Council.

Design & Typography by Relish Design Studio Inc.
Printed in Canada by Friesens

CANADIAN CATALOGUING IN PUBLICATION DATA

Main entry under title:

Norrie, Helen
    He saw himself in all his creatures: a mother's remembrance /
    Helen Norrie.

ISBN 1-894283-63-5

    1. Norrie, Mark.   2. Animals—Anecdotes.   3. Norrie family.
4. Animal specialists—Canada—Biography.   5. Wildlife
conservationists—Canada—Biography.   I. Title.

QL31.N67N67 2006   590'.92   C2006-900500-1

Dedicated to the memory of
Mark Robertson Norrie

1964–2001

*His days were short but each one
was lived with intensity.*

I have a way of surrounding myself with animals. I'd like to think it was animal magnetism, but I don't know if animals are attracted to me so much as I am to them. Whatever the case, wherever I am I accumulate animals of all kinds. It is the animals who find me. I rarely ever buy animals. Instead they come to me injured, orphaned, often sick from inadequate care. And once the word gets out that I enjoy caring for so called "exotic animals" they seem to come in droves!

—Mark Norrie

Prologue

I catch a glimpse of a rabbit scooting across our yard to take refuge in the hedge. But in my mind's eye I see my youngest son, Mark, pursuing that rabbit as a clumsy toddler. He cries with delight as he makes an ineffectual grab for its retreating white tail.

The scene shifts and Mark is now twelve, his mop of unruly blonde curls—that annoy him but delight me—shines in the sun. He is struggling with a long board and a roll of chicken wire. He is off to build another cage.

A chickadee repeats its cheerful song over and over and brings me back to the present. The bird's staccato voice reminds me of Mark's battle to overcome his early stutter. I often thought his passion for animals was partly rooted in that disability. After all, they never remarked on his speech. In fact, when he talked to his animals he rarely hesitated. Maturity and a growth in self-confidence finally defeated that impediment which so plagued him as a child.

I look at the developing pine tree outside my window and think of Mark as a young man. He overcame the scoliosis that caused him to wear a back brace as a teenager and became tall and straight, if never robust. He's wearing a lopsided smile as he tries to urge a recalcitrant wallaby into a pen.

As I glance over incoming mail I remember the hundreds of letters that Mark received from his beloved "Nana", my mother, who corresponded weekly with him for years after he left home. When her eyesight began to fail, around age ninety, she learned to touch type, except she sometimes got her fingers started on the wrong keys. Mark enjoyed "deciphering" the result by substituting the letter to the right or left of the one on the paper. Shortly before her death, at age 100, she wrote her last letter, which he carefully preserved in a scrapbook with her earlier writing. He even wrote a short story called "Bye Now, Love Nana", the way she always signed her letters.

The ruby red hibiscus bloom in my window gives me a final reminiscence. It recalls the last time I visited him, on the tropical island of Bali. He's standing in the Bali Bird Park, with a gorgeous blue macaw and a flamboyant red parrot perched on his shoulders. This is the way I will remember him, surrounded by his beloved birds and unaware of the dark days of depression that were to come. He's smiling, confident and happy—devoted, as always, to the furred and feathered creatures that are in his care.

Salt and Pepper

It began with Salt and Pepper. They were guinea pigs—one white and one black—and Mark's grandfather gave them to him as an Easter present the year Mark was three.

The guinea pigs were round and friendly and intelligent. Within a couple of weeks Mark had taught them to use a litter box like a cat. They also had a cozy basket by his bed, but more often we found the basket empty in the morning and the guinea pigs curled up on Mark's pillow.

Salt, the female, loved to explore, while Pepper, the male, followed her every place she went. They soon had investigated every corner of Mark's room, including every wrinkle and crease in his bed. That was when I had to intervene.

I tried to speak reasonably. "Mark, your guinea pigs don't belong in your bed. They could have an accident. We'll have to move them outside."

"But they'll be cold!" he protested. "I'll watch that they're careful. And how can I play with them if they aren't in my room?"

But we persisted. It was a beautiful morning in May when we carefully transported Salt and Pepper to a wooden box in the backyard. It had once held garbage cans and had a conveniently hinged wooden top that closed tightly but opened easily. Snug in a nest of shredded newspaper and a soft woollen doll's blanket inside a wooden apple box (in the days when wooden boxes were still common) the guinea pigs seemed content to eat and sleep between play times with Mark.

And play times were often strenuous. He soon taught Salt and Pepper to run up and down stairs. It was a comic picture to see two fat, short-legged guinea pigs cheerfully chasing a small, curly-haired little boy from the basement to the second floor and down again. He would call encouragement to his followers as they squeaked in excited pleasure. The guinea pigs also substituted for live cattle in Mark's miniature farm set. They took major roles in the elaborate theatrical productions he acted out with toys and blocks. It was not unusual to see Pepper sitting in the driving seat of a toy fire engine while Mark moved the engine and made siren noises and Salt ran alongside. Or Salt might appear in a doll carriage, dressed in a tiny nightgown and bonnet. When playtime was over they were happy to seek the rest and seclusion of their garden retreat.

Each morning Mark would run outside in his pajamas to check on his precious pets. He usually reappeared with one in his hands and one peeking out of his pajama pocket.

But the morning came when he opened the hinged lid of the wooden box and cried out in surprise. When he was excited he tended to stutter and as he flew back into the house he could hardly get the words out.

"S-S-Salt has s-s-some funny looking little pink things in the nest with her. Are they m-m-mice?"

Mark and his brothers rushed back outside to investigate. I wasn't far behind.

Of course, they weren't mice, but six beautiful newborn baby guinea pigs. Mark's career of breeding and raising animals had begun.

Bambi

There had never been more excitement in our household than the day the director of the zoo phoned to ask if we could nurture a baby fawn. A mother doe had been killed on the highway near Kenora. When the distraught motorist stopped he found a tiny fawn cowering in the ditch beside his dead mother. Convinced the baby was too young to survive on his own the driver carried the quivering young deer to his station wagon and drove directly to the zoo to seek help.

The director realized that the fawn was still nursing, and would require twenty-four hour care. He couldn't spare that sort of help. But Mark's reputation, even at the tender age of four, had spread. Park attendants had noticed the little boy who'd spend hours playing with the animals at Aunt Sally's farm—the petting zoo where children and young animals intermingled. It was rumoured he could nurse any injured bird or animal back to health. Why not ask him to raise an orphaned fawn?

Mark's acceptance, of course, was immediate. Because it was late June and we were preparing to move to our cottage on an island at Lake of the Woods, the fawn would almost be returning home. Coached by zoo staff, Mark purchased baby bottles and special infant formula. Later, he was told, he could introduce him to cut-up apples and carrots. Lacking originality, Mark named him Bambi.

Bambi arrived on the island in a metal cage loaned by the zoo. It was the size commonly used to transport a large dog and fit comfortably into the back of the family station wagon. In anticipation of his arrival, we erected a small corral, consisting of logs about six feet high. Since Bambi was very small, we felt the corral would be sufficient to keep our new visitor safe until he got to know and trust us.

The cage was carefully carried up from the boat as we hovered over it with great excitement. Mark was allowed to slide the door open within the corral and then retreat to allow the fawn to step outside. The other boys, perched on boxes, were hanging over the log siding. My husband Bill and I, and my parents ("Nana" and "Bubba" to the boys) were just as fascinated to see the tiny fawn for the first time. Perhaps it was the effect of this overpowering attention, but the poor creature stepped out, took one frightened glance at his rapt audience, and, in one graceful bound, cleared the top of the corral and vanished into the woods nearby.

The howls of disappointment and despair that issued from our offspring could undoubtedly be heard far across the water. Search parties were immediately dispatched to find the runaway. The centre of the island was thick with pine trees, poplar and deadfall. In the fading light of dusk we tried to push our way through, calling and searching, but it was hopeless. The fawn, well-schooled in the art of blending into the underbrush, had vanished.

That night Mark cried himself to sleep, sure that the woodland orphan was lost forever. Our only consolation was that we were on an island. While deer can swim, we didn't think the little fawn would chance taking to the water so soon.

We need not have worried. At six a.m., as the first rays of morning sun touched our deck, we were awakened by the sound of tiny hoof beats on the stairs. Bambi was back, and looking for his breakfast. A delighted Mark was out of bed in a minute and soon feeding him his bottle of warm formula.

For the remainder of the summer, Bambi would emerge from the woods at regular intervals to guzzle his bottle and then disappear again to a shady spot to rest during the heat of the day. To the amazement of visiting guests, he would sometimes appear when Mark called, especially if he banged the metal pie plate that became his feeding bowl when he switched to solid food.

Bambi also loved to swim and would join in family swim sessions. But when he became tired he liked to rest his front hooves on the shoulders of the nearest swimmer and take a free ride to shore. We tried not to wince as his sharp hooves were suddenly placed on our backs.

By the end of the summer Bambi was a good-sized deer and so accustomed to human company that we were afraid he would not be safe in the wilds, especially in hunting season. He would very likely walk right up to the nearest hunter, especially if he were eating an apple! Now that he was weaned, the zoo agreed to accept him back.

The day we had to return Bambi to the city was a sad one, but Mark was pleased to know that the little deer was going to his favourite area, Aunt Sally's Farm. When we released Bambi into the enclosure he became an instant hit. Children lined up to feed him apples and to pet his inquisitive nose.

For some weeks we paid regular visits to the zoo to check on our adopted family member. At first, Bambi would always come running when Mark called. Then it happened more rarely and finally, when winter came and Bambi was turned into the enclosure with the adult deer, he ignored us completely, happy with his new companions.

The following spring we had another call from the zoo director. "The zoo in Amsterdam has requested a healthy young white-tailed deer for their collection. We think Bambi would be ideal. He's so friendly and good natured. It's a world-famous facility and I'm sure they'd treat him well. Would you agree?"

Mark was at first reluctant but then he agreed that it would be nice for Dutch children to be exposed to a deer as graceful and charming as ours. We never saw Bambi again, but we like to feel that he was an exceptional ambassador in a foreign country.

Sheena

When our family arrived at the Air Canada Terminal one autumn day after Mark's fifth birthday, we were greeted by an unusual sight. Two burly cargo handlers, obviously used to shifting heavy boxes, had opened a small cage and were playing with a minute Yorkshire terrier which could not have weighed more than two pounds.

Mark stared in amazement at the tiny golden-haired pup.

"Mum, is that Sheena?"

The men looked up at Mark's query. "Yep, that's the name on this tag on her neck. You must be the Norries."

Mark nodded and approached the frisky pup with a look of reverence.

"Can I pick her up?" Like the puppy, he was quivering with excitement.

As we signed the forms to acknowledge her safe arrival, Mark scooped up Sheena and placed her tiny nose almost against his own. His brothers, also eager, demanded equal time, but from that moment there was a special bond between the little Yorkie and our youngest son.

Sheena had been born in Scotland in June where Bill and I had first seen her at the age of two weeks. We'd been entranced, and felt that she was just the thing to make our household complete. At the time she was much too young to travel, but now, in September, she was weaned, inoculated, and ready to face the boisterous attention of three enthusiastic young boys.

Like all Yorkies, Sheena had long golden hair, silver at the tips, over most of her body. A shock of darker hair fell over her eyes and the back of her head. She appeared to be always peering through a veil, unless Mark decided to comb the wayward locks into a tiny pony tail on the top of her head.

Shortly after her arrival, autumn leaves began to blanket our lawn. We raked them into a towering pile, but before they could be safely stowed in bags Sheena and Mark discovered their potential for fun. Time after time boy and pup would race through the leaves, scattering them in all directions while Sheena yipped with excitement. Or Sheena would burrow into the pile of leaves until she was entirely camouflaged by their red and gold brilliance, so close to her own. Then she would suddenly burst forth like miniature fireworks as Mark clapped his hands in delight. We decided that raking the leaves again was small compensation for their enthusiasm.

As she became older Sheena became slightly more sedate, but never lost her love of active participation. With her affectionate personality and robust good health we felt she would make an excellent mother. However, when she first came into season we decided she was too young. Every dog in the neighbourhood, and some from the next one, disagreed with us. Sheena's sex appeal was obvious. The pack of would-be suitors hung outside our back door, howling with amorous appeals.

Mark was now enduring kindergarten. He hated to be separated from Sheena and his other pets for a whole afternoon. As soon as he arrived home we would jump into the car; Mark holding Sheena tightly to prevent the unwanted attentions of her lovesick admirers, and drive to a distant park where Mark and Sheena could play in peace. We were often pursued part of the way by barking swains.

The next spring, our first attempt at providing a suitable mate was a disaster. We'd contacted a breeder of purebred Yorkshire terriers who invited Sheena to share a kennel with her champion male. He was smaller than Sheena and she took an intense dislike to him on sight. All his attempts at closer communication were repulsed. Sheena became positively unfriendly. The champion male cowered in a corner. After several hours we removed Sheena before her intimidated suitor was permanently traumatized.

Our second attempt with the good-natured family pet of a friend, also a purebred but much less nervous, was more successful. Some two months later, in September, Sheena delivered four tiny pups in the whelping box we had prepared in my sewing room. As the babies began to arrive, Mark, whom I'd allowed to stay home from school to observe this momentous event, was overcome with awe. He watched with fascination as Sheena opened the tiny sacks in which the babies were born with her sharp teeth before licking her new offspring clean. Once the pups were comfortably settled and nursing, he could barely be restrained from checking on the babies at all hours of the day and night. His constant surveillance, and that of the rest of the family, began to make Sheena nervous.

As an added complication, we had decided to relocate to a larger house. As the moving day approached we worried that the unfamiliar surroundings would bother Sheena and her new family even more. We needn't have worried. Our new home had a basement workroom that contained a cast-iron stove which had been used as an incinerator. With winter approaching and four pups that needed to be trained, it was ideal for disposing of soiled newspapers. The workroom was a perfect place for the new Yorkies. We moved in the little family, Sheena relaxed, and the stove kept the workroom cozy with its daily dose of newspapers.

We were unprepared for the evening we smelled smoke as we sat down to dinner. It seemed to be coming from the second floor and Mark ran upstairs to announce that smoke was seeping out of his closet! A frantic call to 911 brought a full complement of fire-fighters within minutes. Their verdict was swift and surprisingly enthusiastic:

"You've got a chimney fire. Gosh, we haven't had one for a long time!"

"Get the long ladder!" another fireman called, as we watched in amazement.

It appeared that all the paper we'd burned in the cast-iron stove had helped coat an already soot-laden chimney. A small fire we'd lit in the downstairs recreation room earlier that day had been literally the last straw.

Mark's first thought was for our new family in the basement workroom. Rushing downstairs, he grabbed the wicker basket containing the pups and, followed by a concerned Sheena, staggered back upstairs and deposited them in the middle of the kitchen table.

"The firemen might step on them!" he exclaimed anxiously.

And perhaps he was right. Our fire-fighters seemed to proceed from one disastrous move to another. Two men climbed on the roof to try to dowse the flames with shovelfuls of snow. When that was unsuccessful they carried up a large ball and chain that looked as if it had been last used on a southern chain gang. They started to lower it down the chimney to knock the accumulated soot and smoldering debris off the sides of the chimney. Unfortunately, the metal was cold and the roof icy. The ball and chain slipped from their fingers and plunged three stories down to the basement, demolishing the grate in the downstairs fireplace.

Two other firemen hurried downstairs to locate the origin of the fire. We had just renovated the rec room and placed an artificial window on the wall with a mural behind it that looked like the street outside. The firemen took one look at this scene and raised their axes.

"We'll have to break that window and let out the smoke!" one shouted.

Bill, who had followed the men down the stairs, grabbed the arm holding the axe. "Wait a minute," he yelled, "you're in the basement and the only thing behind that window is a wall!"

The sheepish fire-fighters retreated to a higher floor.

When they finally left and the smoke cleared we decided to move Sheena and the pups permanently out of their basement room. The babies were pretty well housebroken and it would soon be time to find homes for three of them. We planned to keep the smallest pup, who was miniature even by Yorkshire terrier standards. Mark named her Thumbelina.

We knew that we didn't need another pet. As Christmas approached Mark came up with the perfect solution. My father had recently retired after fifty years as a teacher and school principal. He was missing the activity of the school and the contact with the students. Furthermore, he was entranced with our smallest pup.

"If we give her to Grandpa then she could still see her mother often," Mark pleaded, "and we could see her all the time as well!"

On Christmas morning Mark decorated a basket with red and green ribbons and placed Thumbelina— similarly bedecked—inside. She became my mother and father's constant companion, and, in the summers, Sheena's favourite playmate at the lake.

Sheena continued to enliven our lives for almost sixteen years. But none were as memorable as those first early days when both she and Mark were youngsters.

Raccoons in the Rafters

Our new home was actually an old house, dating from the 1920s, with three stories and a back stair that had endless fascination for the younger crowd. Our next-door neighbour's home, however, had the added distinction of a garage that had once been a stable for riding horses. It boasted a suite over the stable area with its own wood stove and chimney, probably to keep the grooms warm.

It was the chimney that led to trouble. One spring day our neighbour heard strange noises coming from the roof of his garage. Fearing that squirrels had moved in and would chew the electrical wires he decided to investigate. He found that the noises—mewing sounds not unlike those of kittens—were coming from the unused chimney. When a chimney sweep was finally called he extracted, besides a good deal of ancient soot, three tiny baby raccoons. Their mother had obviously decided that the old chimney made an ideal winter refuge and springtime nursery.

Garbage cans in our back lane had been upset once too often. Our neighbour decided that he had no wish to encourage the mother to return, but neither did he have the heart to destroy the babies. The solution—of course—give them to our son Mark!

Mark was only in grade six, but he had already raised rabbits, guinea pigs, pheasants and a pet fawn. Raccoons were a welcome addition to his zoological adventures.

The raccoon kits, Mark guessed, were only a few days old. Their eyes were still glued shut and their tiny bodies were small enough to hold in the palm of one hand. He received them gratefully, and immediately began to mix up formula which he poured into a doll's bottle. With a little encouragement two of the three babies were soon eagerly accepting this substitute nourishment every three hours. The third refused all but a few drops that Mark was able to dribble down its throat. It grew weaker and died on the second day.

Mark set his alarm clock for every three hours at night and fed the babies again last thing before rushing off to school in the morning. Luckily he was able to come home at noon and was back again shortly after 3:30 p.m.

The raccoon babies soon opened their eyes, began to fill out with round little bellies, and grew a coat of fur, with those characteristic dark circles around the eyes and on the tail. He named the frisky pair Mutt and Jeff.

By June Mutt and Jeff were tumbling about like adorable puppies. They followed Mark wherever he went and learned to eat fish-flavoured cat food out of a dish. They also showed signs of insatiable curiosity! When we discovered that the telephone in the basement recreation room was no longer working the cause was fairly evident. The raccoon kittens had chewed the cord in half. One morning they were missing and turned up inside the laundry chute that ran from the second floor to the basement. They exhibited an incredible dexterity in climbing and opening doors. By the end of the month we were happy to move them to the lake and install them in a large empty aviary where they could explore to their hearts' content.

What we did not count on was the raccoons' agility to use their human-like hands. The first morning after Mutt and Jeff were installed in their aviary, with a strong stick securing the door, we found the stick on the ground and the cage empty. The escapees had not gone far—they had discovered that the beach was full of delicious crayfish and were busy having a raccoon feast.

After several more unsuccessful attempts to keep them secured, Mark finally allowed Mutt and Jeff to roam free. They usually spent part of the day in the aviary in any case, often sleeping on top of an old bird breeding box in one corner. The rest of the time they spent exploring the island, sometimes surprising us as they emerged unexpectedly from the underbrush.

By the time mid-summer came Mutt and Jeff were full-sized raccoons, with distinctive barred tails and dark eyes surmounted by startling white patches. Their capacity for mischief had also increased. No food was safe from their nimble fingers if it was left unattended anywhere outside or near an open window. Garbage cans had to be kept inside; the compost pile had to have a boulder-sized rock anchoring the lid to prevent them scattering the contents all over the septic field.

They also developed a liking for anything with stuffing: chairs, toy animals, cushions on the lawn swing, all had to be guarded or would be found to be ripped apart by tiny fingers. The captivating kittens had turned into the midnight marauders!

The climax to Mutt and Jeff's story came one day when we least expected it. The pair had been trouble-free for almost a week. In fact we had barely seen them for several days—a fact that should have alerted us to danger. Since they were now catching enough crayfish and minnows to feed themselves, Mark didn't have to put food out for his ring-tailed pets, so he wasn't worried when they failed to appear around the aviary.

My husband had some business to do in town and, since he would be bringing back plywood for one of Mark's continuous building projects, he had decided to take the big boat, a twenty foot runabout that was his pride and joy. He was well on the way to town before he heard a series of scuffling noises coming from under the covered bow. When the commotion became more than he could ignore, he stopped the boat and opened the sliding panel leading to the front of the boat. Two inquisitive little faces peered out, playing in a maelstrom of ripped life preservers and styrofoam insulation from the inside of the boat. Like their mother before them, Mutt and Jeff thought they had discovered the perfect hideaway. It also had the advantage of being kept in the boathouse, a location close to their food supply.

My husband didn't share the raccoon's enthusiasm for their new quarters. His lecture to Mark after he had turned the boat around and roared back to the island would not have been acceptable campaign language. It included an ultimatum: Mutt and Jeff had to go!

The next day a sorrowful Mark loaded the two culprits into his own small outboard with a supply of dry cat food and set out for the southern part of the lake.

There, on an uninhabited island, he ate a picnic lunch with his masked pets and then, leaving them to munch on a tasty crayfish snack, slipped away, leaving them to fend for themselves.

We thought that would be the end of the story, but, as it turned out it wasn't. Mark, at the time, had made friends with the local veterinarian. It was less than a week later that the clinic got a call. A couple, picnicking down the lake, had been amazed when a sleek raccoon had climbed into their boat and refused to leave. He seemed to be exceedingly friendly. Could he be someone's pet? They decided to return with him to town.

Mark retrieved Mutt with only faint reluctance. The couple had seen no sign of Jeff, nor did we ever see him again. Mind you, my sister did have a litter of eight raccoon babies in her attic several years later. It's possible that Jeff was just making his presence felt.

The problem of Mutt's residence was solved by a local farmer who enjoyed animals of all kinds. Mutt was given the run of the farm until late autumn, eating large amounts of dog food and growing very fat. One day he curled up in the front seat of an abandoned truck on the acreage and settled down to hibernate for the winter.

The farmer reported that Mutt slept peacefully there off and on for several months. He could be seen exploring the farmyard on mild days but took refuge again in the truck when it turned cold. Then came the day when spring winds started to melt snow in the farmyard. The next time the farmer checked the cab of the truck it was empty. Mutt had taken off to see the world.

Shadow

It was that magical time in early April when your nose tells you that spring is on the way. After a long, cold winter the snow banks had shrunk to grey wisps in places where the sun rarely penetrated and had disappeared entirely where it did.

In our backyard the rabbits had spent the winter underground, snug in a burrow they had dug beneath their wire cage. The present couple were Karl and Kim, Dutch rabbits remarkable for their striking black and white colouring.

As I looked out an upstairs window on that morning when I smelled spring I was surprised to see movement in the rabbit cage. It looked like Karl. This rabbit had exactly the same dark hindquarters and white chest and upper body. But he seemed a little small and remarkably active. As I watched he leapt repeatedly into the air, twirled and twisted and even turned a complete somersault. Karl was an energetic healthy rabbit, but I'd never seen a performance such as this. Then I realized that it was not Karl at all, but Karl's new offspring who had inherited his distinctive markings. We named the little gymnast Shadow.

Shadow was simply the latest in a long succession of rabbits which had come and gone in Mark's menagerie. He had raised longhaired rabbits and shorthaired ones, exotic breeds, miniatures and husky almost-hares. Some had been donated to Aunt Sally's Farm at the Assiniboine Park Zoo. Several had found homes among sympathetic neighbours on our street. But Shadow proved to be the most remarkable rabbit of them all.

He never lost his energy, or his inquisitive nature. When Mark let the rabbits out of their cage after he returned home from school it was Shadow who tried the tempting green dandelion leaves first. He loved to dart across the lawn and hide under the leaves of the rhubarb plant. Mark learned to look there first if Shadow was missing. When we travelled to Lake of the Woods that summer, Shadow refused to stay in his cage. He tunnelled out of every enclosure Mark constructed, even when the wire netting was extended into the ground. Shadow was now full sized, almost 18 inches long, self-confident, friendly, and definitely not shy. He loved to play with Sheena, our Yorkshire terrier, and appeared promptly for food when Mark rattled his dish.

Mark became so used to Shadow's appearances and disappearances that he became careless. He forgot that there were predators on the island who could strike under cover of darkness.

It was a night without a moon when I was awakened by an unearthly sound. It was something between a baby's cry and a soprano's screeching high C. I couldn't imagine what had made the noise but it was dramatic enough to propel me out of bed as if I'd been ejected by a rocket. There was no doubt: something or someone was in mortal terror.

Wearing only my nightgown, I ran out the door and almost collided with Mark, who'd been similarly woken. With the darkness intense, we stumbled our way down the stairs and along the path towards the beach, where the weird sound echoed yet again. As we reached the sand starlight showed us a strange sight. Shadow's black and white form was half submerged in the shallow water, while the sinuous shape of a mink writhed around him, attempting to pull his head under the water.

Mark waded into the water, yelling at the top of his lungs, "Stop! Drop it!" as if he was addressing a dog. As he grabbed Shadow's struggling back legs the mink released its hold and vanished, leaving our poor rabbit gasping for air and streaming blood. Mark cradled his poor, half-drowned pet in his arms. The mink had torn open the skin on his scalp and he was bleeding badly. I felt that he hadn't long to live. We hurried back to the cottage where I wrapped Shadow in a large towel and placed him gently in the bathtub, where further bleeding could do no harm. I finally persuaded Mark that there was nothing more we could do for him that night and we returned to an uneasy sleep.

Next morning I arose early, fully expecting to find that Shadow had expired in the night. Imagine my surprise to find Mark already up, the war-torn bunny nestled in his arms, asking, "Do you think I should feed him, Mom? He seems hungry."

Shadow had not only survived his deadly duel with the mink, but was sitting up looking for breakfast. Later that day, as we received stitches and antibiotics from the local vet, the story of his encounter was told many times over.

"I never heard a rabbit scream before," I admitted, "but it's a sound you never forget."

"And Shadow will sleep in the basket beside my bed from now on," Mark added, "So we won't hear it again."

We never did hear that unearthly sound again, and Shadow lived to a ripe old (rabbit) age. He also fathered many more energetic, black and white babies to take his place.

The Araucana Rooster

M ark's interest in birds had gradually progressed from canaries to cockatiels and finally to outdoor species, pheasants and quail. But it was not until a friend introduced him to Araucana chickens that his interests threatened to disrupt the calm circuit of our family life.

When our friend presented Mark with a clutch of odd-coloured eggs he added a bit of geographical information.

"They're from Araucana chickens," he confided, "from South America. Sometimes they call them Easter chickens because they lay coloured eggs. Maybe you can hatch some."

Mark was enchanted! An opportunity to hatch his very own South American hens! Not that it was his first experience of hatching eggs. He had won a first prize at school when his portable incubator with domestic chicken eggs had delivered four downy chicks on the very evening of the Science Fair. But this was an experiment in exotic breeding. He took to it with relish.

No eggs ever received closer attention. Each one was turned like clockwork according to schedule. He got up in the middle of the night to check that the power was still on. Water was added and the humidistat checked regularly so that there was sufficient moisture. The eggs were guarded night and day from the family dog and from inquisitive, possibly jealous older brothers.

When the eggs hatched, as five eventually did, the chicks were at first a disappointment. They appeared to be perfectly ordinary looking, and as the initial down disappeared all but one of the birds appeared positively dowdy. The exception showed signed of making up for the others, however. He proved to be the only rooster of the group. Soon he sported a tiny red comb on the top of his arrogant head. As his feathers matured they reflected sparks of iridescent green and gold on a background of deep rust.

Weeks went by and the female chicks became rather common brown hens. The rooster's comb, however, grew to a magnificent appendage that he carried like a royal tiara. Sharp spurs protruded from his yellow legs like long, dangerous thumbs. When he wanted to demonstrate his masculinity he would thrust out his chest like a prizefighter and prance around the backyard pen with his four wives in close pursuit. He had one other characteristic that he shared with his more prosaic cousins: a penetrating wake-up call at dawn which was not always appreciated by our long-suffering neighbours. More than one stopped Mark on the sidewalk on his way to school and made pointed remarks about keeping barnyard birds in our backyard. Mark had a ready reply.

"Oh, but they're not *ordinary* chickens, they're Araucana ones from South America!"

That usually stifled the opposition since the puzzled neighbour couldn't think of a quick retort.

There was therefore considerable relief on our street when we departed that year for our summer home at Lake of the Woods. We had a full station wagon: two guinea pigs, four rabbits, six budgies plus, of course, four Araucana hens plus one oversized rooster. On the island the exotic fowl were allowed to wander at will during the day but were rounded up at night and confined to a cage to keep them safe from mink, foxes and other predators. They soon adapted to the routine and returned to their wire enclosure at dusk, where they roosted on plywood shelves that Mark fixed to the sides of the cage.

During the day, however, they roamed the paths that connected the cottages, or pecked their way through the brush, which included some wild fruit trees, spindly birches and the odd pine. One favourite spot was by a stand of wild plums, under which they could usually find a fallen fruit. When they became thirsty it was not uncommon to see a small procession, a harem led by the lordly rooster, make its way down the path towards the beach and water.

My husband, Bill, was walking one morning unconcernedly along one of these pathways near the wild plums when he came face to face with the feathered family. They had just emerged from the shelter of a raspberry thicket and decided to navigate the easier footing of the well-trodden walk. Possibly if both Bill and the rooster had not been completely surprised the result would have been different. As it was, the rooster, on slightly higher ground, launched himself directly at the intruder, his sharp spurs pointing directly at my husband's eyes.

The object of his fury didn't wait around to see if these flying missiles would reach their mark. He reversed his direction so fast that his canoe shoes were left in the middle of the path. Bare-footed, he retreated to the safety of the patio, meanwhile roaring for Mark to come and take care of his "Beastly birds!" By the time Mark arrived the ferocious fowl had settled down and disappeared once again into the bushes.

Meanwhile, the canoe shoes still sat in the middle of the path. When they were discovered there a short while later by our eldest son they provoked a degree of hilarity that was shared by everyone except for my unfortunate spouse. He just could not get the memory of his close encounter with those menacing spurs out of his mind.

"That rooster is a certified menace!" he exclaimed at dinner that evening. "He could seriously injure someone and he has to go!"

Mark would probably not have allowed his father to carry out his threat if he had not been yearning for a new pet, a frisky baby goat. He reluctantly agreed, a week later, to allow the rooster to be carted off the island in a strong cage.

The rooster's absence, it turned out, was only temporary. A month later he was back, but in a state that would surprise, but never threaten. My husband had taken him to the taxidermist, who had given him a merciful end and an immortally heroic image. In all his multi-coloured glory, he sat on a wooden pedestal, chest expended, eyes fierce, one leg raised. It was a pose that would last far longer than his normal life span.

As he stood in his place of honour in the family recreation room he was known to startle guests, an ability that would doubtless bring pride to his rosy breast. And Mark, when he happened to pass through the room, was known to fondly stroke those iridescent feathers on his regal back.

Petunia

It started with an advertisement in the paper. "Baby kids for sale. Phone 334-1212," it read, innocently.

Mark brought me the paper with shining eyes. "Look Mum, baby kids! I've *always* wanted one and I've never had one before!"

The argument was ridiculously familiar. This time I resolved to be sensible and to resist all pleading. "Mark, a kid grows up to be a *goat*! No matter how appealing the babies are the adults are *not*. They're smelly and... (I searched my memory for knowledge of the species) and destructive!" A flash of a long-forgotten experience had suddenly swum, like a buoyant life preserver, to the surface of my mind. I decided that Mark needed a history lesson.

"Have I ever told you, Mark, about the goats on M.L.A. island?" He shook his head, his attention still on the ad in the paper. I pressed on regardless. "Mr. Williams brought down two young goats one summer to help amuse the children. They ate all the petunias and made an awful mess of a box of canned goods that was left on the dock. They were finally banished to St. Helena." (Like the island of Elba, this was a remote Lake of the Woods island suitable for dangerous prisoners.)

Mark refused to see the connection between those long-ago marauders and the sweet baby kid advertised in the paper. "But I can keep him in a cage…or on a long rope," he pleaded. "I'll teach him not to eat flowers, honest!" Mark always had unlimited faith in his ability to handle animals.

Perhaps it was because his animal training skills usually had proven reliable, or perhaps it was that days of repeated entreaties simply wore me down. The next weekend saw us driving into the country north of Winnipeg with a large wire cage in the back of my mini station wagon. We had made one minor change of plan. Rather than heading for the farm of the unknown breeder advertising in the paper, we were approaching the home of a slightly familiar woman who had once sold us a pair of quiet guinea pigs. Knowing she had a wide variety of animals of her "hobby farm" we'd made an exploratory phone call and been assured she had just what we were looking for.

"A kid? Oh yes, I've a six-week-old female that's as tame as a kitten. Just the thing for your son," she'd gushed warmly. We were hooked.

As we manoeuvred our way down a series of gravel roads I found myself repeating a rather apt expression from Shakespeare's *MacBeth*: "I have no joy in this contract tonight…it is too rash, too ill-advised, too sudden." Both MacBeth and I would have been well advised to heed our foreboding.

The "hobby farm", when we finally located it, left no doubt about the nature of the hobby involved. There were animals everywhere! Half a dozen dogs of various breeds, or no breeds at all, ran yelping towards the car as we turned into the driveway. A large orange cat preened itself on the ramshackle fence. A pen full of dirty-looking sheep was visible behind a house that was only in slightly better shape than the fence. A young goat stood perched on a very smelly pile of manure in a second crumbling enclosure. He looked, to my inexpert eye, at least six months old and he was certainly not female. I relaxed when I realized he couldn't possibly be the animal we had come to pick up.

I relaxed too soon. I hadn't counted on the cumulative effect of an experienced saleswoman, desperate to get rid of an unwanted resident, and a determined twelve year-old boy to whom a goat in the hand was worth at least six on a distant farm.

We decided to call him Petunia, in honour of my childhood memories. It was a mistake; he immediately showed signs of identifying with his namesake. I admit that Mark did try to restrain him. First he attempted to keep Petunia in a cage. After the succession of animals we had had on the island, I thought we had accommodation for every conceivable type and size. But we found that the wooden hutches for rabbits were too small and the large, hand-made chicken-wire enclosures (designed for birds) were not Petunia proof. One smart kick of his sharp rear hooves was enough to rip open the chicken wire, even if a sharp head-but to the plywood door didn't release him earlier.

Mark then tried tying a long rope to a tree, sufficient to give Petunia room to leap about a little but not long enough for him to reach the flower beds or the young pine seedlings. Petunia was indignant at this restraint, and his indignation expressed itself in endless bawling complaints at the top of his penetrating voice. These became so constant that boaters would mimic his loud "Maa-aaa-aa!" as they passed the island in hopes (usually realized) of obtaining an answering echo.

Mark and his brothers decided to build a sturdy enclosure where Petunia could be left at night. With eight foot logs that had broken free from former log booms on the lake and foot long spikes holding them together it was an enterprise that required a great deal of labour and considerable time. When it was finally finished the interior was at least four feet taller than the young goat and seemed incapable of being scaled. Mark led Petunia in and left him happily munching on crab apples as he securely locked the gate. We felt a great sense of relief as we watched him settle comfortably down into a pile of hay in the corner. For the first time in days we were able to go to sleep without a chorus of complaints.

We underestimated his ingenuity. The morning after his first confinement we woke to find him on the back patio cheerfully munching on our pots of purple impatiens. As he demonstrated shortly after, he had simply placed his hooves between the logs and scrambled over the top. We were becoming increasingly desperate.

The problem of odour was another matter that had to be resolved. Although our friendly female farmer had assured us that goats never smelled until they were physically mature, ours was apparently precocious. The expression "to smell like a goat" obviously had legitimate origins. The trouble was that everything that touched Petunia, which included, of course, Mark, had the same strong stench. We tried baths—both for Petunia and for Mark—but it didn't help the first and was strictly temporary for the second. Mark tried sprays: "essence of lilac", "fragrance of pine". But aside from causing Petunia to go into fits of sneezing they had no apparent effect. In despair we sought veterinary advice, but instead received a lecture on the inadvisability of choosing goats as pets. We were no closer to solving the problem.

Things came to a head one day when we were absent from the island for several hours. We had left Petunia tied securely to a young pine tree. As we approached the island we noticed there seemed to be a new ornament in front of the living room window. As we got closer we realized it was Petunia, trailing the end of his chewed rope. He was happily swallowing the last of my father's prize begonias.

If there had been some problem buying a goat it was nothing compared to the difficulty of getting rid of one. Even Mark had by now admitted that Petunia was not a desirable pet. That didn't mean, of course, that he would allow anything drastic to happen to him. When a visitor casually mentioned the popularity of roast kid in several Mediterranean countries and cast a meaningful eye at Petunia, Mark was outraged.

"You wouldn't, you *couldn't* do that to Petunia!" he gasped. I agreed that much as I would like to, I could not.

The matter was finally resolved when we heard about a small petting zoo located a few miles out of town. The owner was quite glad to get a clean young goat donated. We decided to make the transfer quickly before he could change his mind.

When we had settled Petunia in a corner of a pseudo-rustic corral Mark threw his arms around him and gave him a long, last hug. He responded with an affectionate lick of my son's ear, but I noticed that his eyes were already looking speculatively over Mark's shoulder. I turned to see what was attracting his attention. It was a beautiful bed of rose-coloured geraniums just beyond the corral fence. As we turned to go, Petunia was licking his lips.

It's for the Birds

Despite his love for animals of all kinds, Mark always had a deep affection for birds. Perhaps it was their vulnerability that attracted him, besides their beauty and cheerful companionship. Whatever their appeal, he was seldom without at least a pair of budgies (properly called budgerigars), with usually two or three cockatiels, at least one parrot and once a beautiful blue macaw.

On the island he built large aviaries of 2 by 4s with chicken wire sides and tops. Inside were growing trees, small spruce and poplar that soon sprouted through the wire ceilings. The trees provided excellent perches while wooden nest boxes fixed near the ceilings offered a sheltered environment for hopeful parents.

Regrettably, the chicken wire did not prove impervious to predators. One morning in July Mark appeared holding a shivering yellow cockatiel that I recognized as one he had named Sunshine. When I examined him more closely I realized why he seemed off-balance. The unfortunate bird was missing its right leg. He had apparently been roosting close to the edge of the nest box when a mink or rat had climbed the wire and tried to pull him off his perch.

Mark took the cockatiel to the veterinary clinic where he was working part time that summer. Here he acquired the nickname of "The Bird Man" because of his skill with feathered clients. However, a missing limb was beyond his talent. The veterinarian stitched up Sunshine's wound, applied antiseptic, and assured Mark that the bird would probably adjust to his disability. She was right. When Sunshine was returned to the aviary (now reinforced with heavier wire and with a strong metal "do not climb" barrier at the base) he proceeded to quickly make his way to the top, using his beak to steady him while he reached up with his remaining leg.

Sunshine lived to a ripe old age for a cockatiel. His name mirrored not only his colour, but also his disposition. Sunshine looked on the bright side of things and he taught us that one should never let a small matter, such as a missing limb, interfere with the enjoyment of life.

* * * * *

Jonathan, a seagull named after his famous literary relative, was another bird who was brought to Mark in an injured state. The seagull, which had probably had a too close encounter with an eagle in a fight over a fish, had lost the principal feathers from his left wing. As a result, trying to fly resulted in Jonathan cartwheeling into the water or ending up on his side in the grass.

Mark received the unhappy gull from a neighbour at the lake, who found it trying to hop to safety on her deck. The poor bird was quivering with fear as Mark took it gently in his hands to examine it. Retiring to a quiet spot beside the aviaries, he stroked the gull gently as he assessed the extent of his injuries. The bird seemed to respond to his treatment. He stopped quivering and settled peacefully into Mark's hands. Then Mark did a surprising thing. Holding the bird firmly with his left hand, he pulled out the three longest feathers from his right wing. Jonathan stretched his wings and shook himself. Then he tried a short flight. Amazingly, he no longer cartwheeled, but flew straight and level, if lower than normal.

Jonathan seemed to feel that he had found a friend. He stayed close to our island for the next couple of weeks, by which time his feathers had grown back. Then one day, when a whole flock of gulls were fighting over a fish out in the bay, he launched himself into the middle of the fray, seized a morsel of fish and spiralled high into the sky.

We never saw Jonathan again, but my neighbour never ceased to use the incident as an example of the importance of balance.

"Emotions are like pinfeathers," she'd point out to her grandchildren. "If they're tipped too far in one direction you'll be miserable. You need to keep an even keel, just as that seagull needed to have his wings balanced in order to fly."

* * * * *

Misty, a small blue budgie, taught us our final lesson. Mark had hand-raised Misty from a new-born chick in the nest-box, feeding him every few hours with an eye-dropper. Misty responded to all this attention by being extremely tame and approachable. As a result, Mark kept his cage in the kitchen and let Misty move in and out of the cage as he wished during the day.

Misty enjoyed perching on the top of the curtain rod over the window, where he could vocalize with the songbirds outside, or preen himself as he viewed his image in the glass. He also enjoyed sitting on the counter close to the telephone, where he would scold us if we talked too long, or attempt to join in the conversation.

As a result, Mark was surprised to find him one day on the floor by the refrigerator. Afraid that he might get stepped on, he lifted him back to his perch near the window. However, the next time Mark came into the kitchen Misty was again on the floor.

This happened several more times until the day that I opened the refrigerator door and found that here was no light, and no evidence of cooling. The fridge had simply stopped working. Because it was relatively new I suspected a mechanical defect and called a repairman, who arrived next day. Pulling the fridge out from the wall, he looked closely and then grinned.

"I think I've found the problem. Do you have mice in the house?"

"Heavens, I hope not!" I replied, surveying with dismay the chewed wire that he'd removed from under the frig. Then it hit me. Misty! "Could a bird have done that?"

I indicated Misty, regarding us ironically from his perch atop the nearby curtain rod.

The repairman laughed. "Certainly! He looks innocent, doesn't he? But we get lots of calls from people who own birds, or hamsters, gerbils, pet mice, even rabbits. They all like to chew—especially if they're a little bored."

After the wire was repaired, Misty was banished to Mark's bedroom. A miniature playpen was installed in the bird cage—a swing and a bell that at first proved very popular. But soon Misty began to once again sit despondently in his cage and to peck at his feathers until his neck became almost bald. Mark decided he needed a companion, which led to the arrival of Perky, a pretty female budgie with bright yellow plumage. She immediately absorbed most of Misty's attention and his feathers soon grew in again to their usual glossy fullness.

We had learned a final lesson: boredom is dangerous, even in birds. Not only humans need the companionship of a member of the opposite sex! The next spring Mark was excited to find his nesting box occupied. The tiny fledgling that emerged after some weeks was blue with yellow feathers on his wings, a perfect mixture of his proud parents.

Lo Tsen

Mark had just finished reading *Lost Horizon* when a ferret was brought into the Veterinary Clinic in Kenora. The animal had been found hiding in a garden. She was emaciated and frightened, but with her "long slender nose, high cheekbones and egg-shell pallor of the Manchu" she was the image of the delicate Chinese princess in James Hilton's novel, at least in Mark's eyes. He immediately named the ferret "Lo Tsen" after the character in *Lost Horizon* and decided to take her home.

Lo Tsen had not only a long slender nose, but a long slender body. She could insert herself into the tiniest of holes. Once she adapted to our cottage, her natural curiosity asserted itself. It wasn't unusual to reach for a stick of firewood from the woodbox and find Lo Tsen peering out at you from behind the next piece of kindling. She also liked to check out canned goods in the pantry. Perhaps, with her acute sense of smell, she could determine their contents, or possibly she simply enjoyed investigating unfamiliar objects of all sizes.

Her favourite spot, however, was in the front of Mark's sweatshirt, where she loved to curl up and sleep while he worked with his animals and birds. The two-legged and four-legged creatures on our island became fairly used to Lo Tsen. Her distinctive fragrance, a musky odour that refused to disappear despite repeated baths, usually betrayed her presence before she was visible. Her inquisitive face with its short creamy white fur which darkened to almost coal black near the back of her head would suddenly appear above the neck of his shirt and then, just as quickly, disappear again as she sought the warm hideaway below.

It was after we left the lake and Mark returned to high school that Lo Tsen precipitated a crisis. I doubt if Mark had intended to take her to school that day. It had simply become so commonplace for him to allow her to ride inside his shirt that it barely registered that she was there.

He entered his typing class that morning and took his usual seat in the back row. Typing was one of those classes that required little concentration. You simply had to repeat exercises endlessly until the key sequence became automatic. As innumerable quick brown foxes jumped over equally prolific lazy dogs his thoughts drifted to plans for a new indoor aviary in his bedroom.

The teacher, whom we'll call Miss Parson, also regarded the class as a necessary chore. She strolled absent-mindedly up and down the aisles. Now and then she stopped and corrected a line of typing or commented on a student's skills. She reached Mark's desk and bent over to check his progress. Unfortunately, Lo Tsen took that moment to wake up and stretch her aristocratic neck out of Mark's sweater, directly below Miss Parson's nose.

The teacher's scream stopped every finger in the room and brought a janitor, working in the hall outside, to the door within seconds. Mark leapt to his feet and Lo Tsen, of course, disappeared.

Miss Parson, now backed up against the blackboard, her face as white as the chalk, regarded the lump in Mark's sweater with horror.

"What *was* that Mark—that creature who wanted to bite off my nose?"

When he was excited or stressed, Mark still had a tendency to stutter. This was definitely a stressful moment. "P-p-please Miss P-p-p-Parsons, it's only Lo Tsen. She wouldn't have bitten you. She's a S-S-Siamese ferret and she's very *tame—really!*"

The other typists by now had recovered from their first alarm. "It's only Mark!" the girl behind him assured them. Someone began to laugh. Mark's menagerie was a well-known fact in the school and many of the students had known him since elementary classes. Soon the whole room was convulsed. The teacher remained unamused.

"Well, whatever it is, I suggest you leave the class now and get rid of it!" she demanded. "And don't come back until it is *very* far away!"

Blushing furiously, Mark gathered his books and made a hasty exit. When he arrived home early that afternoon he quickly retired to his room. It was only much later, at a parent-teacher interview, that the day's events became clear to me. I had to make profuse apologies and promise that Mark would never be allowed to let his ferret enter the school again.

By that time my husband had also had an unpleasant surprise from Lo Tsen. Turning to his filing cabinet one day to search for a folder, he almost jumped out of his chair when she poked her head out from among the files. His shout could be heard a block away.

"Mark, come and get this dreadful weasel (Bill was never sure of species) out of my study! And don't let me ever see it again!"

Mark decided that life would be calmer, and possibly safer, for Lo Tsen in a different household. It was with regret that he said goodbye to his Chinese princess as he carried her to her new home with an elderly lady who had recently lost her pet cat and was amenable to a new adventure. At least, he mused, *his* Lo Tsen was saved from the premature aging that overtook her namesake in the novel. Lo Tsen was exotic and mysterious, but she was, after all, only a ferret.

Gourmet Offspring

When Mark was in high school he received a gift of a dozen fertilized quail eggs from an enthusiastic fellow breeder. Having already nurtured Araucana chickens as well as domestic hens, hatching quail eggs was a cinch!

Quail are small, perky birds about half the size of an adult chicken. They adapted easily to our outdoor aviary and didn't seem to mind sharing it with some older prima donnas in the form of exotic peacocks. When summer came Mark transported them all, without much difficulty, to his aviary at the island.

The chief problem of keeping quail on the island turned out to be preventing mink, fishers and other predators from attacking at night when the birds were roosting. The chicken-wire sides to the aviary proved too easily breached by the enemy and the quail began to disappear one at a time. With only six of his miniature fowl remaining, Mark constructed a sturdy wooden hen house that could be locked at night. The disappearances stopped. As an added bonus, four of the remaining quail began to lay eggs.

Quail eggs are small, about half the size of a hen's egg, and are highly prized by gourmets. While I could never detect much difference in the taste of a quail egg from that of an ordinary domestic hen, culinary experts disagree. They maintain that if you hard-boil them, extract the yolk and garnish it with mayonnaise and herbs and then reinsert it, they make an appetizer if not fit for a king at least guaranteed to excite astonishment. So it was that Mark's lowly quail were to play an important part in an event that coming autumn.

In September, with school dictating a move back to the city, Mark moved his menagerie to Winnipeg, complete with half a dozen quail. The hens were now laying their speckled eggs with admirable regularity. We took to keeping a few dozen eggs in the refrigerator at all times, ready for exotic omelets or fluffy sponge cakes.

Cooler weather arrived in October and Mark closed in his backyard aviary with plywood and a little insulation. We suggested it might be time to move the quail to a friend's farm outside of the city but Mark was determined to keep them as long as they were laying eggs. As it turned out it was lucky he did.

On the first Friday in November a major winter storm hit Winnipeg. Snow began falling heavily in the early morning and by evening most streets had become impassable. Buses stopped running; the airport closed because the snowplows couldn't keep the runways clear. Only children were delighted and hurried outdoors to construct forts and snowmen.

On Saturday morning I received an urgent phone call from a close friend. Her son was planning to be married that afternoon. The bride and several of the wedding guests had arrived from out of town before the blizzard hit and were staying at their home. However there was no way they could get to the church or to the hotel which had been booked for the reception. Could I ask my husband, who was then Winnipeg's mayor, if the city planned on plowing Pembina Highway, a major thoroughfare and the location of their proposed reception, before the afternoon?

With the city on emergency status because of the storm, Bill had been picked up by a front-end loader at eight o'clock that morning and transported to the "war room" at City Hall. I managed to get a call through to the Commissioner of Public Works. There was no way, they told me regretfully, that Pembina Highway could be cleared before the next day. Inner City main streets had to be plowed first. It was also doubtful that the streets surrounding the church would be clear before late in the afternoon.

When I reported back to my distraught friend she made a quick decision. Since most of the wedding guests were scheduled to fly back to their jobs Sunday evening, provided the airport was clear, the ceremony couldn't be easily postponed. She decided that the wedding must go ahead but would be held at home, providing the priest could get there by snowmobile. Wedding guests were contacted by phone and those who lived close enough agreed to don snowshoes or cross-country skis to make the trip. One even offered to play the wedding march on the piano.

The bridesmaids were luckily all members of the family and already in residence. One main avenue, a few hundred metres from the house, had been plowed open and guests were able to make it to a spot at the end of the street by taxi if they were willing to struggle through knee-deep snow to the front door. That left the problem of the reception.

The groom's mother pleaded for any available refreshments. As I began stirring a quick-mix cake, I thought of the three dozen quail eggs sitting in the refrigerator. Mark wandered into the kitchen to see what all the phone calls were about. He had a cockatiel perched on one shoulder and was preparing to venture into the backyard to check on his shivering fowl.

"Quick Mark," I ordered, "Put a large pot of boiling water on the stove."

He looked shocked. "Why? Are you going to have a baby?"

"Of course not!" I snapped. (He had obviously watched too many pioneer movies). "I want to boil the quail eggs."

This made about as much sense to him as preparing for a baby, but he did as I asked. After I had explained about the wedding emergency he even helped prepare the quail eggs by mixing the seasoning into the hard-boiled yolks.

By noon, assisted by cross-country skis, we were able to deliver the completed appetizers and cake, plus a six pack of beer, to the wedding household. We were in time to help with final preparations for the ceremony. The bridesmaids had decorated the house with Christmas lights and pine boughs. They'd even found some silk flowers for the bride. The priest did arrive on a snowmobile and several hardy guests plowed their way through the snow. It was one of the most memorable weddings I have ever attended.

It also began a legend in the neighbourhood. Who else but Mark could supply three dozen quail eggs as appetizers for a wedding on four hours notice?

Ginger

It may seem unlikely, but a few of Mark's animals gained fame, like Sydney Carton in *A Tale of Two Cities*, not so much by living their lives as by leaving them. Ginger was one of these notables.

Ginger appeared without warning one day in a cage that Mark had previously used for rabbits. He was medium sized, rosy-coloured, and very definitely a pig. He looked soulfully at us. (We later discovered this meant he was hungry.) When we asked Mark where on earth he had found him he was somewhat evasive.

"I just discovered him…he needed a home and you know, pigs are said to be very intelligent and to make excellent pets…I'll train him to follow me like a dog…and they aren't really smelly…the book says they're really clean!" As Mark paused for breath we shook our heads in disbelief. But Mark had the ability to convince anyone that he could perform miracles with animals of all kinds.

Ginger, unfortunately, had not read the same book. The only talent he exhibited was an ability to follow Mark around. In all other respects he proved disappointing. His level of intelligence appeared distinctly low. Mark tried in vain to teach him tricks, or even to come when he was called. We decided that, like humans, pigs have a range of intellectual powers and it wasn't Ginger's fault that he had ended up at the bottom of the pig scale.

He did have one more distinct ability: to eat. It certainly cut down on the amount of kitchen waste for the composter. He would happily consume as many scraps as we fed him. Left-over hot dogs, orange peels, the remains of last-night's stew, all were welcome to his indiscriminate palate. Mark was kept busy carrying delicacies to Ginger's pen.

It also took all of his efforts to keep his pen sweet-smelling. It had to be cleaned at least daily and even then, after a rain, Mark would find that Ginger had soiled all the straw by wallowing in the mud in a corner. Despite the fact that he knew this was natural behaviour for pigs, Mark found Ginger's mud baths difficult. It meant he had to lead him down to the water in the morning and try to wash off the results of his evening activity.

After Ginger had been with us for a few weeks Bill had to attend an agricultural conference in Winnipeg. He was surprised when he was approached by a man with the tell-tale ruddy complexion of a farmer, but whom he was sure he'd never met.

"How's my pig doing?" was his surprising opener.

Bill was confused. "Do you mean Ginger?" he asked.

"That what he called him? I guess he was sort of ginger-coloured. I mean the pig I sold to your son a few weeks ago."

Comprehension dawned! The pig that had been "discovered" had been discovered on a farm, doubtless as a result of an advertisement.

"Why he's doing quite well," Bill managed to reply, meanwhile thinking how he would confront Mark with the story of this encounter. "He seems a little....well, not too bright, if you know what I mean."

The farmer laughed. "Oh, that breed of pigs got all the colour and none of the brains. Three meals a day they'll finish off...more if you feel like it. Fatten 'em up and send 'em off to market, that's what I say."

When Mark heard the story of Bill's coincidental meeting with the farmer from whom he'd bought the pig he was suitably contrite.

"Sorry Dad, but I was afraid if I told you where I'd bought Ginger that you'd be upset. I mean, I know that

I have a lot of animals on the island right now (this was an understatement) but I'd never had a pig and I really wanted to see what they were like."

This was a familiar argument and one which we'd given up debating. Besides, Ginger had become "one of the crowd" and we accepted his presence on the island as a natural—along with the birds, the ferret, the rabbits and the exotic chickens.

For the rest of the summer Ginger provided entertainment for visiting children, who loved to come and hang over the wooden logs which made up his pen and feed him apples and cookies. Perhaps it was these extra supplements, but he also grew to an immense size, far outstripping the rabbit cage in which he'd arrived. By the end of the summer he was almost too big to fit in the boat.

Once again Mark turned to the local vet for assistance. Did she know of any farmer who would like a pig? Luckily, she did. On the Labour Day weekend Mark managed to deliver Ginger to a farm only a few miles outside Kenora.

"He was really glad to get him!" he reported to us. "He looked him over very carefully and seemed pleased."

We were relieved. Mark had managed to dispose of Ginger and sooth our consciences at the same time.

It was several years later, after Mark had left home, that the vet sent us a one-page chart on Ginger that she had found in her records. Besides mentioning her initial examination and several inoculations when Ginger had been first brought in, it had a final succinct comment in Mark's handwriting.

"October 3rd. Sold to farmer for Thanksgiving dinner." Mark had not been as naïve as we thought. Ginger had made the supreme sacrifice.

Joey

When Mark first saw Joey he was hardly bigger than a large mouse. A man had found him cowering in a corner of his boathouse and brought him to the Vet Clinic. He wasn't even sure what this sleek, dark-skinned animal was. The vet confirmed that he was a baby otter, but so young that he'd need bottle feeding if he were to survive. Of course, Mark offered to foster him, and named him Joey, the name given to young kangaroos, because of his strong, fleshy tail.

Joey slept in a basket beside Mark's bed at night and often travelled in his shirt pocket during the day. At an early age Mark introduced him to the water—in the bathtub. He was surprised to realize that otters have to be taught to swim, but Joey was soon slipping through the water with surprising agility. Then came the day when we all gathered at the beach to watch Mark introduce Joey to the lake. We were somewhat apprehensive as he carried the young otter, now over a foot long, to the shore. Would Joey simply dive into the lake and swim away? Would he recognize his natural habitat and disappear?

Mark placed Joey gently in the shallow water next to the shore. With an ecstatic leap, he dived under the surface and swam several feet under water, only to surface again with drops of water clinging to his impish face and bristly whiskers. Mark described this experience in a story called "The Swimming Lesson".

> *Lively dark eyes sparkled as his small sable head poked out of the water. Beneath a small, stubby nose, long grey whiskers trailed aimlessly in the water. Tiny ears lay flat against his head and he continually called to me with a curious bird-like chirp. Soon, however, the great expanse of the lake seemed to overwhelm him and the little animal scrambled up on my shoulders, crying piteously. For a long time he stayed there, clinging determinedly to my neck while I tried to swim. But gradually his courage increased, and he started taking short expeditions, always returning to his human perch when he grew nervous.*

With Joey sometimes on my shoulders and sometimes in the water beside me, I proceeded to swim right around the small island on which my family's cottage was situated. Along the shore, massive pine trees loomed majestically. Above us, framed against a cloudless blue sky, seagulls soared, screaming raucous cries. Finally, without warning, Joey's true ability and confidence emerged, and he began swimming in a graceful, undulating motion. It was dolphin-like and very fast.

Instantly, Joey was everywhere: speeding past me like a furred torpedo, diving through my legs, floating on his back in front of me, circling around me like a shark. His raw energy was incredible; his sheer joy undisguised.

That was only the start of Joey's introduction to the lake. In the days that followed, as he gained independence and confidence, Joey made his own way to the beach in search of crayfish. If anyone should attempt to swim while he was nearby he was a ready companion, suddenly appearing underwater or describing circles around the bewildered swimmer. Mark described how unnerving this could sometimes be:

Periodically, he would disappear for a split second, during which time I would receive a playful nip at a toe or two. Before I was completely aware of what had happened, Joey would be beside me again, appearing always shameless and innocent. My swim shorts were not immune to playful assaults either, and with persistent tugs, Joey more than once succeeded in pulling them down to my knees. I made a mental note to be sure to wear shorts without an elastic waistband, if in future I ever swam with the otter in female company.

Joey followed closely behind as I climbed up the ladder onto the dock. Immediately he pulled my towel off a lawn chair and slid across it repeatedly. Having exhausted its benefits but still remaining slightly damp, he proceeded to rub his sinuous body against my legs. Before long the imp was thoroughly dry and I was left wetter than ever—with a soaking towel.

Joey never tried to swim away. Obviously, Mark was the only mothering influence he had ever known and he wasn't about to become an orphan. Sometimes he would swim out to boats which were anchored close to our dock, fishing for walleye. One pair of fishers became so used to Joey's visits that they would whistle when they hooked a small fish and Joey would leap into the water and swim out to claim his treat. The fishers in the bay laughed as he wiggled his appreciation of their left-over scraps.

Joey communicated by a series of sharp chirps, rather like those of a chipmunk. One day we were surprised to hear a whole series of chirps emanating from the boathouse. Joey had found a family of wild otters and was cavorting riotously with them. But later that day when the otters had moved on, Joey re-appeared at Mark's feet.

That year Mark, who had finished high school, elected to stay at the lake until late in the fall.

"I won't be lonely," he assured us as we left to return to the city. "I'll have Joey to keep me company."

As the days became shorter and fewer anglers visited our bay, Mark allowed Joey to roam farther afield while he worked on his writing in our treetop studio. One day he was surprised to find that Joey had not returned at nightfall. He called, whistled, rattled Joey's old food dishes (unused for weeks since he had discovered crayfish) but got no response. That night his bedside basket was empty.

The next morning Mark set out to call on the few neighbours who were still in residence. The first two couples, who had watched Joey swim, fish and play all summer, had no suggestions as to where he had gone. The third lived on the other side of our island. They had only recently arrived from the States and hadn't been aware of Joey in the summer. Their words made Mark turn white.

"Yes, we saw an otter yesterday. It climbed right into our boat after we'd been fishing." The man's voice was strained. He'd obviously been afraid. "We were frightened. We knew that wasn't natural behaviour. When we jumped out of the boat on shore he started to follow us up the path!"

Mark tried to contain his emotions as the man paused.

"I'm sorry. You say he was your pet? I had no idea. We thought he was rabid! I grabbed a gun and shot him as he ran behind my wife."

We mourned for Joey, the lively, playful companion who had enlivened our summer. But he also taught Mark a valuable lesson: that making any wild creature dependent on you and unafraid of humans is courting disaster.

Mark retrieved the limp body of Joey from our American neighbours, and buried him beside the grave of Sheena, our loyal Yorkshire terrier who had died the previous year. When he returned to the city, Mark decided to move into his own apartment and attend the University of Winnipeg. His chief problem was in deciding which of his assortment of birds and animals he could take with him. His new landlady had some surprises in store!

The Punch and Judy Affair

I f truly "the best surprise is no surprise" then we never experienced that blessed state in all the years that Mark lived at home. With his obsession for adopting unusual pets, we suffered through goats who feasted on our petunias, a ferret who slept down the neck of his t-shirt, raccoons who crept into our boat and chewed the insulation, and many more mischievous, if not downright destructive, pet animals.

We therefore experienced a sense of some relief when the day arrived, at the age of nineteen, that our son felt sufficiently affluent, or possibly anxious to be free of parental supervision, to look for his own apartment. We assumed that this would write a firm "finis" to the saga of creatures and calamity, but we were wrong. We had not anticipated what came to be known as "The Affair of the Pygmy Hedgehogs".

Mark managed to find a small apartment on the second floor of an old house. His landlady, Mrs. McNeil, was a hardy Scottish woman who was not unfriendly, but who believed a little physical discomfort was good for the soul. As a result the winter temperature on the top floor never rose above fifteen degrees centigrade and hot water was only available from six until nine in the evening.

The suite, however, did have other advantages: a small enclosed sunroom, for instance, on the south side, and its location in a quiet residential neighbourhood. It was accessed through a door on the ground floor that concealed steps leading upstairs.

Since Mrs. McNeil had incautiously agreed that "I dinna mind a bird or two", Mark moved into the apartment with only his feathered friends: a pair of rosella parrots, two cockatiels and four budgies. Their home became the sunroom. Fortunately, since parrots and cockatiels are not notoriously quiet, this was at the back of the house, out of range for sleepers at the front. The apartment seemed the perfect accommodation.

Several months went by, and it seemed that both Mark and the birds had adapted well to the new surroundings, when the Pygmy Hedgehog craze hit.

As we had observed many times before, Mark could never resist a new species of pet. When, upon his arrival at the lake the summer before with a rusty coloured piglet, we had asked in amazement, "Why on earth did you bring a pig?" he had simply replied, "But Mum, I've never had one."

This year, however, the most popular new inhabitant of all the local pet stores was the pygmy hedgehog. Unfortunately, Mark had to pass a pet store every day as he walked back and forth to the university. He soon decided that his life was not complete without one of these unique companions.

These prickly little creatures are about the size of a large grapefruit, but much more difficult to hold. While not sharp like porcupine quills, their spines are hard and bristly, and not even babies of the species could ever be described as cuddly, though they can fit into your hand. Furthermore, being nocturnal, they tend to sleep most of the day and become active and interesting only after most of their owners are asleep.

None of these disadvantages deterred our son, however. He acquired a pair of these new stars of the pet world, named them Punch and Judy, and proceeded to install them in a little cage in a spare closet, without permission of Mrs. McNeil.

The hedgehogs were not much trouble. Mark would let them play in the kitchen as he cleaned their cage after he got home from classes. He even claimed they had distinct personalities, with Judy being much more aggressive.

Mrs. McNeil, by now, was not quite so indifferent to what Mark kept on the upper floor. The cockatiels, it seemed, had woken her several times from pleasant afternoon naps with shrill screeches that even her Presbyterian conscience found unnecessarily irritating. She began to regret her offhand comment about "not mindin' a bird or two".

It was one night when Mark was asleep that the hedgehogs, doubtless led by Judy, managed to push open the door of their cage and set out to find some excitement. When Mark woke in the morning and went to say "Good Morning" to his prickly pets, he found the door ajar. A frantic search ensued, but they were nowhere to be found. Starting at the cage, he began a systematic, desperate exploration of the apartment. It wasn't large, but it had plenty of corners and cubby-holes big enough to hide a pygmy hedgehog.

Finding not even a trace of the escapees, he finally thought of checking the coat closet which was located at entrance to his suite. As he descended the stairs in a bound, he thought he heard a tiny squeak from one of the overshoes. He pounced on the suspicious hideout and found both hedgehogs peering up at him with innocent eyes. That was when there was a knock at the door and he recognized his landlady's voice.

"Are ye there, Mark? I need to have a wee look in the hall closet!"

Calling a hurried excuse, Mark snatched up the boots containing the escapees, rushed back up the stairs and deposited them, boots and all, back in their cage. He then descended the stairs in two jumps and opened the door with a breathless apology that he was barely out of bed. Given the fact that he was still in pajamas, this seemed reasonable.

"Mark," enquired Mrs. McNeil, "I'm ver-r-ry afeered we may have some mice!" (she pronounced it "meece"). "I coudna sleep last night fer their scratchin's. The noise of it seemed to be comin' from yer closet here."

Belatedly, Mark realized that his hall closet backed onto Mrs. McNeil's bedroom. He knew he should make a full confession but the survival of his beloved hedgehogs appeared to be at stake. Perhaps he could avoid direct disclosure until he could remove them from the premises.

"I'm sorry, Mrs. McNeil," he replied with what he hoped was an earnest expression, "but I've seen no mice. But please feel free to look in the hall closet."

After Mrs. McNeil had left, Mark rushed to the phone and dialled our number.

"Mum, I'm sorry to bother you, but do you think you could look after Punch and Judy for me for a few days until I could find them a new home?"

I wracked my sleep-befuddled brain for a few moments to remember who Punch and Judy were. So many pets had come and gone in our home that it needed a computer to track their names and genealogy. Then the light dawned. The pygmy hedgehogs—surely small enough to be kept in a corner of Mark's old bedroom. I agreed and the tiny trouble-makers arrived before lunchtime.

The Punch and Judy Show, however, had not quite run its course. Possibly Mrs. McNeil had her suspicions, because conditions at the apartment continued to become more difficult. The hot water ceased to function at all. Visitors after nine o'clock in the evening were forbidden. Mark was not allowed to use his stereo. Finally, at the end of the month Mrs. McNeil announced that she wanted to take over the upper floor to store extra things. Perhaps she could move some of her clothes upstairs at once? She had noticed there was a spare closet. (It was the one, although she did not know it, that the hedgehogs had only recently vacated.)

While it was hardly convenient, Mark, perhaps feeling guilty over the Punch and Judy affair, was reluctant to object. He had become disenchanted with living on his own in any case. (He said he never realized how much toilet paper and soap could cost). As a result, we soon had not only the hedgehogs, but a son and several birds again in residence.

I felt rather sorry for Mark, being evicted from his first private "digs". He was relaxing in his old room one day with a brilliant yellow cockatiel on his shoulder when I walked in to sympathize.

"That wasn't very considerate of Mrs. McNeil to ask you to move out in the middle of winter," I suggested, "Perhaps you should have asked to stay?"

"Well, I found it rather cold there for my animals anyway," he replied seriously, reaching up to stroke the cockatiel, which was now pecking at a button of his shirt, "And anyway, I feel a little sorry for Mrs. McNeil."

"Really? But why?" I asked in surprise.

"Well, you know," he confided, "She brought up all her clothes and a musty old fur coat to that closet just before I moved out. I didn't want to tell her that I might have left something behind."

I was still mystified. "What do you mean," I asked, "Did you forget something?"

"No, not exactly," he sat up and balanced the cockatiel on his finger, "You see, pygmy hedgehogs are notorious for having fleas!"

Kotare

Mark spent ten months in New Zealand after he finished high school. Visiting the country on a Rotary exchange scholarship, he attended three different schools and lived with three different families. The first family had three boys, who attended a private school based on the English model. The model, however, seemed to be out of the time of Dickens. Mark found the excess of rules and regulations stifling. He much preferred his third placement, on a sheep farm where there were plenty of animals to interact with, and he was allowed to attend the local public school.

Mark returned from New Zealand with a slight "down under" accent, a dislike of private education and an intriguing geographical name which he soon bestowed on a new dog: Kotare.

Kotare was a cross between a German shepherd mother and an unidentified father. Whatever her patrimony, she had inherited the complete loyalty and intelligence of the shepherd along with an impressive physique. Mark found Kotare at the Winnipeg Humane Society and immediately brought her home.

It was spring when Mark first introduced us to his new dog. Luckily, as Kotare was energetic and powerful, she could sleep outside in a hastily-built doghouse that Mark constructed. But she didn't sleep much. True to her shepherd ancestry Kotare loved to herd any animals which happened to be loose around the yard. This could include rabbits, guinea pigs, and the occasional neighbour's cat. This hardly endeared her to our neighbours, but Kotare was so good-natured about her attentions that even the cats came to accept her. She even made friends with Mark's latest ferret and they could often be seen tumbling together in the grass.

At the lake that summer Kotare shone. She loved to ride in Mark's fourteen foot outboard boat, standing on the front seat like a Viking ornament with the wind streaming past her expressive face and lifting the collar of white fur around her shoulders. Mark often took Kotare to work with him at the Veterinary Clinic that summer, where she would lie, surprisingly quiet, under the desk where Mark was working.

When children visited the island Kotare was in her element. She would swim after thrown sticks for hours or join in the children's games of hide and seek. When they went swimming she would join in, though she sometimes got into trouble trying to "rescue" ones that she thought had swum out too far.

Mark had another pet with him that summer, and one which caused some controversy. It was a young skunk named Punky whom he'd rescued from being put to sleep. We did insist he have Punky de-scented, and while this prevented any unwelcome outbursts it never completely removed the musky odour that was Punky's natural smell. Kotare, however, in her good-natured way, had become used to Punky and allowed him to play around and over her while Mark was working.

Mark elected to stay on the island that year after we returned to Winnipeg. He was working on his writing and still filling in part-time at the Veterinary Clinic. With Kotare at his side he assured us he'd be fine. He had friends in Kenora he could call if he wanted company or needed any help.

Fall that year was exceptionally mild. Bright warm days were followed by crisp, calm nights. When we returned for the weekend at Thanksgiving the poplar and birch trees had turned a brilliant canary yellow. The beavers had stepped up their efforts to fill their lodges (one unfortunately under our boathouse) with a winter supply of branches. We departed, reluctantly, after the weekend, taking with us two budgies and a cockatiel for warmer indoor climes.

After we left Mark and Kotare roamed the lake, discovering hidden beaches and exploring old portages that had been hidden by summer foliage. Mark spent hours writing in the upper story of our guest house, with a window looking out on the branches of the pine trees, with Punky and Kotare curled up beside him on the floor. It was like a rediscovery of Thoreau's wilderness.

Then, on Hallowe'en, as if in response to a ghostly decree, the temperature dropped. Wisps of snow could be seen around corners of the cottage. Mark awoke one morning to find the swimming bay iced over. He also found a frantic message on the answering machine from us. "Mark, you must come home! There's a major blizzard warning for tomorrow! Find a parka, wrap up your animals and get off the island right away."

He was still reluctant to leave. He'd dreamt of staying on the island all winter. Surely this was a temporary squall. He could ride it out. The final and successful appeal came from my mother, Mark's much loved "Nana". As he told us later she'd phoned him with a stern message; "Mark, if anything happened to you on the island, how could any of us enjoy going there ever again? You must come home."

By the time Mark gathered his remaining animals (Punky, a few rabbits and Kotare) and made sure they were snugly stowed in his boat, the weather turned nasty. As he turned north towards town around the corner of our island he saw a wall of approaching snow that was being swept towards him from the north. Within minutes he couldn't see the land. It seemed just as bad behind him so he pushed on, sure that at least no one else would be on the lake and he wouldn't run into another boat. Kotare left her place in the bow and snuggled under a seat. Mark found his eyelashes were freezing together and he couldn't see. The trip which usually took fifteen minutes stretched to almost an hour. Finally there was a short break in the swirling snow and he glimpsed the Keewatin Bridge ahead of him. He had made it to the mainland!

By the time Mark arrived in Winnipeg there were over 25 centimetres of snow on the ground and traffic was slowing to a crawl. Before the next morning another twenty centimetres fell, causing streets to be shut down completely. He and Kotare had made it home just in time.

But now there was a new problem. The doghouse was covered in snow and besides, Kotare had become used to sleeping indoors on Mark's bed. She didn't want to be left outside, and the increased cold made it dangerous for her.

Bill insisted that Kotare was too large, too energetic, and with her wet fur, too smelly, to live in the house. As the cold increased we compromised. Kotare was allowed into the "mud room", a small area inside the back door. Mark was miserable, and so was Kotare.

Things came to a head around Christmas, as Bill bawled out Mark for trying to sneak Kotare up to his room. She got loose, only to knock over the Christmas tree. We found her cowering amidst the ruin of smashed ornaments and squashed presents. As we surveyed the damage it seemed that my husband's patience with Mark's menagerie had finally worn out.

The solution came from an unexpected quarter. Mark decided to move to Victoria after Christmas. He found there was a Creative Writing course in the Faculty of Fine Arts with well-known authors such as Peter Newman. He could transfer credits from the University of Winnipeg and enroll in second year. But there was one drawback. He would need a small apartment and he couldn't take Kotare with him.

The second part of the solution was a case of happy coincidence. A woman with a severe hearing loss, who happened to be distantly related, had just lost her constant companion, a black Labrador dog. She heard about Mark's problem and asked if he would consider leaving Kotare with her. When he took Kotare over for an introductory visit Mark realized it was the perfect place for her. Here she would not only be loved and cared for but she could exhibit all her caring instincts as she helped guide her mistress across busy streets and alert her to dangerous sounds. Reluctantly, but gratefully, he agreed to leave her behind.

Kotare became a legend in her new home. Not only did she go everywhere with her new mistress, including to university classes where she lay under the seat while the professor talked, but she became a real part of the family, sleeping beside her mistress's bed. She watched over her as carefully as she had once watched over the rabbits in our backyard. She had found her true vocation as a shepherd!

The Winter of the Wallabies

When the day came for Mark to actually leave for Victoria, he was laden down with luggage. It seemed essential to him to take as many household items as possible; after all, he didn't want to have to buy sheets and pillows, blankets and dishes in Victoria. But of course he also had his birds—two cockatiels and several finches in an antique metal cage. Suitably covered, they were allowed to ride with him in the cabin of the plane. In addition, he was adamant that he couldn't leave Punky behind.

"People don't understand about skunks" he argued, "They're afraid of them. None of my friends will take him. (I could see their point!) If I send him to the humane society, they'll just put him to sleep. I'll have to take him with me."

He did agree that Air Canada might have reservations about transporting a skunk, even a de-scented one. His solution was to find a closed-in cage that allowed only a glimpse of the furry animal inside. The cage he marked in large letters, "CAT". All that was visible was a small bit of white fur from Punky's centre stripe. Fortunately no one became curious and he travelled to the West Coast without any problem.

When Mark arrived in Victoria he was lucky to be able to rent a small, basement apartment in a central part of the city. It had a large hall closet which, with the door removed, he quickly converted into an indoor aviary. Punky, who fortunately never made the aquaintance of the landlord, took up residence in the bedroom. When he got loose on a visit Mark made to Lester B. Pearson College of the Pacific, Mark was unable to locate him. He had to leave him behind in the pine forest. He sometimes wondered if the students at the college had been surprised (or shocked) by a friendly skunk wandering into their dormitory.

Mark enjoyed his classes at the University of Victoria and found a part time job at the Crystal Garden, the large indoor facility near the Empress Hotel that was formerly a swimming pool but was converted into a zoological garden with birds and small mammals. Here he was in his element, surrounded by tropical birds, miniature monkeys, ring-tailed lemurs and Indian fruit bats. Unfortunately the Garden has since been closed by the British Columbia government. Mark enjoyed caring for the birds and animals and working as an interpretive guide for school groups.

After classes ended that year he took a job as a public relations officer with the provincial government. The position required that he spend the summer in Nanaimo, some one hundred kilometres north of Victoria. He enjoyed the change of scenery and liked the semi-rural atmosphere of Nanaimo, especially after he met a contractor who had property outside the city. The contractor had dreams of developing his land into a retreat, complete with a stream and ponds and a place for animals and waterfowl. Mark was enchanted. It was as if his lifelong dream of having a place for all his animals had come true! But he had to convince the owner of the property that he should be allowed to move in and participate in the project. It is a testimony to his powers of persuasion that before the summer had ended Mark was living on the land outside Nanaimo, having given up his studies in Victoria and moved, birds, animals and all, to the house which was now under construction.

To support himself, Mark was induced by friends to take a realtor's course and participate in the booming real estate business that was taking place in Nanaimo at the time. What his friends and advisors hadn't counted on was that Mark was constitutionally unfit to try to sell anyone anything. Day after day he sat in his cubicle in the real estate office trying to get up the courage to make "cold calls" on prospective buyers or sellers. He marvelled at the agents who arrived at nine o'clock sharp and by ten had made over a dozen calls. He was contemptuous of the ones who avidly read the obituaries each morning and phoned the survivors, pretending to be members of the same service clubs or social groups as the deceased, offering to be of assistance in selling their property. He tentatively showed a few properties to former friends from Victoria or ex-Winnipeggers seeking warmer weather. But sales were few and Mark was miserable.

Wallabies, however, were what saved Nanaimo from being a complete disappointment. Mark learned that these ungainly, miniature cousins of Australian kangaroos were surprisingly hardy and could easily survive outside in the relatively mild climate of Vancouver Island. He set about obtaining a pair from the state of Washington.

When Mark approached the immigration officer at the border south of Vancouver with papers for a pair of wallabies he was met by reluctance and resistance. Why did Mark want to bring these strange Australian animals into Canada in the first place? Was he sure they weren't dangerous? Yes, he had veterinary certificates but what if they had some strange "down under" disease that hadn't been diagnosed? (It didn't matter that they had been born in the US.) Where was he going to keep them? How big would they grow? Were they endangered? Finally Mark was able to convince the officer that the baby wallabies he had packed into cotton pouches in the back seat of his car would not be a threat to Canadian citizens. They waved him on his way and Mark added "wallaby raiser" to his list of previously sheltered animals.

While he was building cages for the wallabies on the property outside Nanaimo Mark allowed them to enjoy the comforts of indoor living. The female, Flora, was timid and quiet. She readily accepted the bottles of special milk which Mark offered her several times a day. The male, Wally, was a different story. He early on demonstrated the ability of his powerful hind legs to leap up on the coffee table in the living room to watch television. He preferred horse pellets, apples and hay to the feeding bottle. When he was taken outside for a run he circled the property in leaps and bounds and disliked coming back into the house. It was a blessing to all when the outdoor cage was completed and Mark was able to move the wallabies outside.

The "Winter of the Wallabies" proved to be an exciting one, with several other females acquired from Canadian breeders, which eliminated border disputes. Eventually, the following Spring, young ones began to arrive by natural means. Due to the uncommon breeding habits of wallabies, which have only about a month gestation period but another six months of babies living in the pouch, Mark sometimes found it difficult to tell which females had "joeys", or offspring in the pouch, until a small furry head would poke out. He soon had a whole group of these energetic and often amusing marsupials to care for.

When we visited Mark that summer we were amused and entranced by the antics of his extended family of wallabies. Wally, his first male, still enjoyed watching television. When released from his outdoor enclosure he would make a bee-line for the glass doors of the family room, hoping to catch a glimpse of the T.V. set inside. The little joeys were adorable, like furry piglets from *The House at Pooh Corner*.

But Mark had found a new interest. He wanted to study dolphins. At the end of that year he applied for an Explorations Grant from the Canada Council, asking for funds to finance travel to view the endangered dolphins of Nepal and China and to write about them. The Explorations Grant, a now-cancelled program, encouraged projects which involved exploration and discovery. With the help of the writing which he had completed in Victoria, Mark obtained the grant and prepared to leave Nanaimo. Most of the wallabies were sold to other enthusiastic breeders, with just a few left for the enjoyment of the good-natured contractor.

Mark wanted to travel to China first to see the sacred white dolphins of the Yangtze River. Then he proposed to fly to Bali, Indonesia, where he felt the Canada Council grant could be stretched to its limit, allowing him time to complete his proposed novel.

We were excited by Mark's successful grant application and interested in his plans to relocate to Bali. What did we know of this tropical island? Very little. Like Mark we envisioned waving palm trees, curving beaches, and gentle people. Bali had all these things, but it also had a darker side.

But as Mark said goodbye to Wally and Flora and his family of wallabies, financial problems and difficult decisions were far from his mind. He was off on a great adventure, one in which dolphins would star!

Dolphins

It was probably inevitable that Mark, who had talked to animals all his life, should eventually decide to study dolphins. He knew that scientists believed them to have a distinct vocabulary and that, in the future, a person would decipher it. Possibly he dreamed of being that person.

Mark had another reason for wanting to study freshwater dolphins. He knew that they were an endangered species and he had always wanted to study the idea of extinction. At the age of twelve he had written a futuristic story about a young girl who was fascinated by pictures of whales, which in his story had become an extinct species. His writing continued:

> *The little girl stared motionless at the whale depicted on the shiny page and, in only a few seconds, realized the beauty and importance of*

this magnificent mammal that generations of people before her had failed to see. Even though she was only a child, she realized that the disappearance of the dinosaur was natural, since it had died along with its environment. However, the disappearance of the whale she knew was a crime because it had been exterminated from a world in which it still belonged, a world it had as much right to as those who had finally killed it.

Fresh water dolphins are an endangered species which exist only in certain rivers in China, Nepal and India. Bill and I were planning a trip that fall by boat down the famous Three Gorges of the Yangtze River. We wanted to see this famous waterway before the largest hydro-electric dam in the world flooded the banks. Mark decided to join us after learning that in Wuhan, where the boat trip ended, lived one single dolphin or baiji, rescued from an accident with a fisherman in the river, and kept in a freshwater pool.

In an article he wrote at the time called "The Eyes of Extinction" he said:

There is a special significance for me to the Three Gorges Project, a personal connection which fuels my obsession with the Yangtze and its dolphins. Ten years ago, shortly after his graduation with a masters degree in civil engineering specializing in water resources, my older brother, Duncan, worked on the feasibility study for this project. From his desk in Niagara Falls, Ontario, and without ever having been to the dam site, he calculated figures, plotted graphs, and formulated tables which would eventually impact the lives of 1.3 million people forced to relocate because of the dam, not to mention the millions of non-human organisms which wouldn't have such luxury.

Over the years, innumerable family holiday dinners ended with Duncan and I stalemated in an embittered debate concerning the ethics of a project with such profound human and ecological implications. We weren't alone in our differing views. From its original conception by an American engineer in 1940, the Three Gorges Project has been surrounded by controversy, both in China and around the world. The intense debate continued until April 3, 1992, when the National People's Congress voted to proceed with the project.

My brother was elated. As much as I didn't agree with him, I couldn't help but admire Duncan's conviction. He viewed water and all of nature as a resource, something to be utilized, harnessed and altered to suit human needs: to him it was so clear and simple. Four months later, while flying into Kathmandu, where he was supervising a feasibility study for a major Nepalese hydroelectric project, Duncan's plane crashed in the Himalayas. He died, thirty-three years old, without ever having seen the Yangtze River or the Three Gorges. My journey, therefore, is a pilgrimage for us both: an opportunity for Duncan to see, through my eyes I hope, the Yangtze River and the construction site of his beloved dam, and for me to witness the baiji while they still exist.

Our trip down the Yangtze River lived up to all our expectations. Because we were on a local tour boat, most of the other passengers were Chinese. In the evenings, after darkness extinguished the towering walls on either side, the plantations of mandarin oranges that lined the less rugged slopes, and the temples and statues that would be flooded by the rising waters, Bill and I learned to play mah-jong. Our clumsy attempts to excel in this ancient Chinese amusement proved hilarious to most of our fellow voyageurs. Mark, meanwhile preferred the cleaner air and star-filled skies of the upper decks.

His recollections of this experience will give a clear picture of how it affected him:

I wake the second day on the river at 6:30 a.m. An intercom is blasting an incomprehensible Chinese announcement in my ear. Assuming we must be entering Qutangxia, the first gorge, I join the stampede upstairs and reach the top deck as a pink hue is beginning to seep through heavy mist. Gradually, sheer limestone cliffs are delicately revealed on either side of us. Ahead, the river seems to trace through this fracture in the earth like a snaking brown vein. I am filled with an eerie feeling of familiarity. I have been here before. I have seen all this before, countless times, in famous photographs and in brush strokes on paper and silk. As the sun rises I stand on the deck in awe, watching the magnificent scenery unravel like an ancient scroll.

We arrive at the second gorge in the afternoon as the sun is starting to set. My guide book states Wuxia, Witches' Gorge, is famous for its twelve peaks and each has a name related to its form. From the excitement around me, it is obvious the other passengers can see images my unimaginative Western brain can not.

Climbing Dragon, Sage Springs, Facing Clouds and Fir Tree Cone all elude me, appearing only as bare rocks. But as we continue past the sheer cliffs I begin to see figures high above. Congregated Immortals Peak does look vaguely ghost-like and Assembled Cranes and Flying Phoenix somehow resemble birds. When we reach Goddess Observing the Clouds, the most famous peak, I am excited. In the fading light framed between two pastel clouds, I can actually see a stone maiden kneeling in front of an altar. Suddenly I understand the mysticism of the place which has inspired Chinese artists for centuries.

We enter Xiling Gorge at six a.m. next morning in the dark. I sit by my window worrying I might somehow become distracted and miss the dam. When the construction site finally comes into view an hour and a half later I laugh. This moonscape of rock, mountains of gravel and Mechano Set of red and yellow cranes would be impossible to miss. It engulfs everything in its path for miles, eating into the hillside behind and leaving gaping open wounds which glare in the sunlight like mirrors. When completed, enough material to build forty-four Great Pyramids will have been dumped into the river, creating a structure the height of a 60-story building.

I climb to the top deck carrying a metal ruler I have brought from Duncan's drafting kit at home. It seems small and insignificant now, but it is all I have, so I stand in silence for a few moments, then toss the ruler overboard, watching it fall quickly into the murky water below. When I turn around I am met by a crowd of confused and concerned faces. Further on, we pass the project's name printed in enormous red Chinese letters on shore. Hard as I try I cannot feel the resident spirit of this place. To me there is not any sort of magic here—only concrete and rock.

When we dropped Mark off in Wuhan he did indeed manage to see the freshwater dolphin which is kept there in the Institute of Hydrobiology. On his second day at the Institute the scientists lifted the dolphin out of the water for its regular monthly checkup. He wrote of his experience in being at the pool:

The eyes of extinction I have witnessed are smaller than the head of a thumb tack, disproportionately minute and almost useless, the legacy of a discarded sense from a former era of evolution. They belong to a baiji, a Chinese river dolphin, the most endangered dolphin species in the world, and some scientists claim, the most endangered large mammal.

This specific animal, the only one of its kind in captivity, exists in a small, perfectly round concrete pool. It is protected from natural elements by concrete and glass, protected from water pollutants by pumps and filters, and protected from the human race by wrought iron fences and padlocked doors. It is so valuable that the Peoples' Republic of China has designated it a Living National Treasure. It is so rare that it is kept in isolation, tucked away in a fenced compound amidst vacant buildings, like a priceless antiquity locked in a vault in the dusty bowels of a museum. It has been catalogued this way for sixteen years.

While the scientists work and the animal lies completely still, I kneel next to him, my hand resting lightly on his body. The experience startles me. No matter how hard I try, I cannot discard the feeling that this creature is the last of his species. I know this is not true, some baiji do exist in the wild, but the air in this building is air I have never breathed before. Now I know the air breathed by the last Tasmanian wolf to die in captivity, and the last passenger pigeon. Throughout the earth's existence, billions of organisms have evolved only to meet extinction. But how many of them have spent their last days surrounded by concrete, behind padlocks, slowly suffocating? I hope very few.

Mark knew that the completion of the Three Gorges Dam would spell the end of the freshwater dolphins in the Yangtze River. Already highly polluted, additional silt gathering in the lower reaches of the river would make it too dense for even the surviving dolphins, already blind from the viscous water, to endure. Musing on the concept of extinction he wrote:

Extinction is not what I expected. I thought it would feel like death, however, this presence was not death. Death is more sudden, more irrational, more sad, yet ultimately more hopeful. Even in death there is a sense of rebirth. Despite individual mortality there are offspring to carry on the genes of the species. But extinction is not like this. There is no offspring, no hope, only futility; an ominous and persistent air of inevitability. The feeling is emotional but it is not sad. It is deeper than sadness. More pathetic.

It was this connection between death and extinction that Mark hoped to explore in his writing in Bali. Possibly this was a subject that would prove too painful, too difficult, and ultimately, too dangerous. In the eyes of the baiji he had seen the cessation of hope, the knowledge of its own tragic destiny. Did Mark transfer these feelings to his own life? Did he come to believe there is an inevitability in extinction?

Possibly. All we know is that when he looked into the blank eye of that Living National Treasure he wrote these words:

The most remarkable part of gazing directly into the pupil of a baiji is that it is solid black. The effect is a perfect mirror. In it, I see my own reflection.

Bali Hai's...

When Mark first arrived in Bali he spent several months living in a rented room on the outskirts of Ubud, Bali's artistic centre, while he worked on his writing. In his spare time he explored the woodworking compounds, the art galleries and the fabric markets that abound in the town.

Naturally, he was also drawn to the Bali Bird Park, which boasts over 1,000 birds, from rare Bali Myna Starlings to more common peacocks. He took to visiting the Park several times a week, and was on the spot when the curator, a woman from California, announced that she had decided to return home. Mark had worked with tropical birds in the Crystal Garden in Victoria. He had raised parrots and budgerigars, finches and canaries, even a macaw and a cockatoo. He decided to apply for the job. To his surprise and delight he was accepted.

With the prospect of a full-time job, Mark decided to look for a more permanent home. He found one for rent, suitably remote, on the side of a hill running down to the river. It was half way between Ubud and the Bali Bird Park, the perfect location for a fledgling Park curator. After a brief visit home, where we shared his excitement over his new job, he moved into his new quarters.

Mark found another advantage to his new house: it had a most obliging landlord. He didn't object to the multitude of cages which sprang up like mushrooms outside its walls. In fact he even brought his children to admire the birds and animals which Mark bought to take up residence there. They admired the many coloured birds, laughed at the antics of the sugar gliders, and hooted back at the small ape, Sammy, which swung back and forth in a cage beside the roof of the house.

A few of the animals were allowed to roam free. A pair of mandarin ducks settled comfortably on the small pond Mark had built on the slope below the house. When he added a miniature deer some months later it was content to stay beside the pond under the shelter of a large palm tree. The deer was light brown in colour, dainty and agile, and mute, except for a distinctive barking noise which it made when it was upset. Mark named him Silka.

In the pre-dawn hours one morning Mark was asleep in his second storey bedroom, which covered the whole top floor of his house. His wide windows were open to the heavy-scented tropical night air. Suddenly an unfamiliar sound disturbed his dreams. As he sat up in bed he realized it was the miniature deer barking frantically.

Mark rushed to the window but the semi-darkness obscured everything in the forest below the house. He almost slid down the stairs to the main floor and in another few leaps covered the concrete steps to the pond. The sight that greeted him was one beyond even the reaches of his fertile imagination!

Behind the trunk of the large coconut palm cowered Silka, still barking relentlessly, despite the quivers of fear which shook his small body. In the pool one of the ducks swam desperately in circles trying to avoid the creature at the side of the water. On the side of the pond lay the other duck, lifeless in the tightening grip of a giant python.

Mark lifted the panic-stricken deer in his arms and carried him to safety inside the kitchen of his house— one of the few rooms with a secure door. He then managed to catch the remaining duck and find a place for it in one of his cages. The python remained coiled by the pond. By now it had managed to swallow the unfortunate duck and was digesting its meal.

Morning brought activity to the household. An old woman appeared and replaced flowers on the Hindu shrine outside the door of the house, a ritual she performed every day. The houseboy, Made, appeared, ready to clean cages and feed the animals. Mark immediately tried to get him to help capture the snake by the pond. He was unprepared for his reaction. Made's face was a mask of horror as he caught sight of the python. He turned white and ran back up the stairs, not stopping until he reached the gate at the top above the house. Pythons, it appeared, were untouchable, taboo. No reasonable person would venture near them, let alone try to capture one.

Mark, however, where living things were concerned, had never been reasonable. Besides, he argued, if he were to leave the python free in the tropical forest surrounding his home, how could he ever let Silka or any of his birds or animals free anywhere nearby? What about Kopi, the stray dog he had adopted only the week before? He would never be safe with a giant python in the vicinity.

Later that day, with the help of a muscular neighbour who was not a native of the island, he managed to wrestle the python into a wooden box and transfer it to a large glass cage with a slotted cover, a former aquarium. Still lethargic from its early-morning meal, the python curled up in a corner, content to doze in saturated slumber.

For the remainder of Mark's time on Bali he was the only one who could approach the python. Fortunately, the snake ate rarely and seemed content to sleep most of the time. But neither Made nor any of the Balinese who worked for Mark would ever go near the cage. Did they know something Mark didn't know? Possibly these simple people, whose religion is close to the earth, knew that ever since the Garden of Eden the snake has been a mortal enemy of man. In any case the arrival of the python heralded the beginning of Mark's "summer of discontent".

And Lows

A job in a tropical bird park, a house in the jungle surrounded by exotic birds and animals, an idyllic climate amid beautiful scenery: it seemed too good to be true, and it was.

The day came when Mark faced a number of unpleasant truths. His job at the Bird Park had come to an end—largely through his own demands. The salary was minimal, but it was sufficient as long as he lived modestly. But Mark was not a modest person. He bought handcrafted furniture for his new house and antique stone Buddha's for the garden. His beds were covered with Balinese hand-painted quilts, his walls with original paintings of birds.

For his collection of living things, nothing was too expensive. He sent letters of enquiry to South Africa regarding exotic cats; to California for scarlet macaws, to a breeding farm in Canada asking after wallabies. Most of these inquiries came to naught, but he still spent hundreds of dollars on birds and animals, some of which turned out to be sickly and died before he could even get them settled. More money was spent on cages, on his *koi* pond, on building a fountain in the garden. By the winter of 2001 Mark was not only broke but heavily in debt.

He also had to face the fact that he had made little progress on his book. Despite his good intentions, furnishing his house and caring for his multitude of creatures left little time for writing. Besides, social life on Bali was always active and sometimes frantic. Many of the young men and women who lived there were independently wealthy, or, like nineteenth century "remittance men", living on money sent "from abroad". They threw lavish parties, dressed extravagantly, and travelled widely.

Mark wanted to reciprocate. He spent his last savings on a spectacular party for his thirty-sixth birthday, complete with costumes, gourmet food and wine and six stalwart Balinese natives who carried him in on a platform. As the local gossip writer commented, "It was the party of the year!"

But now Mark faced the consequences: no job; no money; no book.

From the distant reaches of Canada, the answer seemed obvious. Return to his city of birth and start again. Possibly go back to school, get a degree in zoology or animal psychology and prepare for a further career with animals. Of course he would have to sell or give away his menagerie and cancel the lease on his house but surely those were trivial matters? We would send him a return ticket to Vancouver.

What we had not realized was the deep connection that Mark had made with the house in Bali and with the birds and animals with which he had surrounded it. How could he leave the little bit of Paradise that he had made in the Balinese jungle? What would become of his beloved animals: his dog, Kopi; his white cockatoo, Snowdrop, that sat on a perch on his front porch; Silka, the beautiful deer who had survived the attack of the python? He couldn't face the idea of giving them away.

And then there was his pride. He'd had everything he had dreamed of, and it had seemed to disintegrate into dust. He'd entertained many friends at his home in Bali. They had all been envious of his beautiful furnishings, his charming "mini zoo", his apparently easy lifestyle. How could he face them as a failure?

Mark could not bear to part with it all. He chose to stay in Bali forever.

* * * * *

When we learned of Mark's death we flew immediately to Bali, a flight that lasted almost a day and a half. Once we arrived it was a nightmare that involved dealing with hysterical staff, stoical police, a superstitious landlord ('very, *very* bad Karma'), and incredulous friends. While we sought to come to terms with our own grief we also had to fend off avaricious animal dealers who wanted to carry off the more valuable creatures in his collection. The days passed in a blur of misery and frantic sorting out of both his affairs and his belongings.

Most of Mark's birds and animals were given to friends: the birds to the aviary of a local hotel where the keeper was an acquaintance, Kopi to a special colleague. Silka was spirited away in the back of a friend's station wagon minutes before an animal rights activist tried to claim her. She went to a safe and spacious green space on the outskirts of town. We even had to arrange for the python. A nearby reptile farm agreed to add her to their collection.

Sammy, the small ape was claimed by the police. It seemed that Mark had neglected to obtain a special license for its containment.

Many pieces of his handcrafted furniture were sent to his brother's home in Vancouver, a few to our summer home at Lake of the Woods. A special case was the stone Hindu shrine which sat in Mark's garden. It now rests in his brother's backyard in Vancouver where it can still have flowers placed on it all year.

We were left with the most precious legacy of all: Mark's journals—hundreds of pages of his life story, and of his thoughts, his regrets, and his hopes. In one of these Mark wrote the following quotation from Eesha Upanishad:

> *Of a certainty the man who can see all creatures in himself, himself in all creatures, knows no sorrow.*

Did Mark see all his creatures as part of himself? Certainly he made no differentiation between the needs of his birds and animals and his own requirements. In a sense he gave his life for them, because he could not bear to leave them.

We indeed hope that Mark, who saw "himself in all creatures", knows no sorrow.

Epilogue—the Visit

I remain undecided about reincarnation…after all, reincarnation also involves going backwards, and I could be reincarnated as a Balinese dog—a fate wished on no one. Nevertheless, every day I am in Bali I make an offering to the Gods to thank them —and every day I am not in Bali I still make an offering to the Gods to bring me back to Bali forever.

I raised my eyes from these words in my son's journal, and looked out on the tropical scene beyond the large windows of his study. Since it was on the second floor of his rented house, I was on a level with green coconuts hugging the trunk of a palm tree. Below were the roofs of many enclosures for his collection of exotic animals, the pool he had built for his miniature deer, and the profusion of aviaries for tropical birds of all colours. I realized that the scene was full of sounds: the soft voice of the young Balinese woman feeding fruit to Mark's pair of emerald green parrots, the twittering and chirps of finches and starlings, the deep hoots of Sammy, his pet ape.

It was literally a world away from the island at Lake of the Woods in Canada where we had received tragic news. We could hardly believe that our youngest son had died, by his own hand, at his home in Bali. It was such a peaceful spot that he had chosen five years earlier to research the increasing loss of endangered species, especially the rare Bali Myna starling. After working in the Bird Park he had found employment at an Elephant Safari enterprise. But suddenly, his dreams of founding a refuge in Bali for endangered animals were wiped out, along with his life.

As I listened to his tame cockatoo whistling outside the study window I reread the words in his journal and thought about reincarnation. What did I know about it? The rebirth of the soul in another body? A superstitious Hindu belief? Or a spiritual mystery hidden from cynical Western eyes but revealed to true believers?

I turned to another passage in his journal: "Made tells me I am 'tamuh'—a unique foreigner who is in the process of being reincarnated as a Balinese. This is the highest compliment he can pay me, as the Balinese believe they are a chosen people." Did this mean that for my son reincarnation might be possible?

When I left Bali, with its exotic scents, its gentle people, its verdant landscapes and its mystic mountain, Agung Guning, which dominates the horizon, I left these musings behind. The idea of any sort of renewed existence for the individual spirit seemed a delusion. Death was final; horribly and inexorably final. It must be faced in all its bleak and unforgiving reality.

But later, when I returned to the lake and to the island where my son spent so many happy summers, the idea of a departed soul finding rebirth through nature seemed less ridiculous. One day I saw a brilliant monarch butterfly on a hazelnut bush and I recalled an Aboriginal legend about butterflies being the manifestation of lost spirits. I found myself praying, "Just let another butterfly land on this branch. That will be a sign that my son's soul is at peace and has found joy and beauty like this butterfly." But the butterfly flew away and no new one appeared.

On a night shortly afterwards I stood outside marvelling at the brilliance of the summer sky. It was the time of the annual meteor showers when you can often see flashes of celestial brilliance overhead. Once again I silently prayed, "Send me a sign! A shooting star—just to let me know that you are still part of this vast universe." But there was no burst of answering fire, and the stars seemed fixed firmly in their places.

As the days of August slipped into cooler evenings and earlier sunsets, I realized I would soon have to return to the city. If my son's spirit was indeed captured in the rocks and water of the island, as I felt it must be, then it was not something I could see or know. Then, on the last day before we were to leave, an amazing visit occurred.

My mother, who was in her hundredth year, was lying half-asleep on the sundeck, while I was busy painting some distance away. She was awakened by something nudging her foot, while she was stretched out on a lawn chair. As she opened her eyes she was startled to see a half-grown bear cub standing at her foot, solemnly regarding her. Struggling upright and groping for her cane, she tried to call out but found she was speechless. By the time my mother got to her feet, the cub had turned and calmly made his way down the nearby stairs.

Watching in amazement, my mother saw that there was another bear at the foot of the stairs. It was larger, but not huge, and appeared to be looking up at her as she clutched the railing around the sundeck. Then, as the cub reached its side, it turned and they both disappeared down a path into the woods. Aroused by a final startled cry from my mother, I was just in time to see the larger bear blend into the underbrush.

The strangeness of the visit; the lack of fear or aggression on the part of the bears, the audacity of the cub who had climbed the stairs and nuzzled my mother's foot, all filled me with wonder. I could not help thinking—of course! If my son were to be reincarnated in *any* form it would not be as a frivolous butterfly or as a cold streak of light. It would certainly be as an animal—he who loved all animals with a passion that was almost an obsession! He also loved a good joke, and loved to dress in costume. What a *marvelous* joke it would be if he suddenly appeared before his beloved grandmother, with whom he had had a very special bond, and who had corresponded with him faithfully every week for ten years.

And the second bear? What of our older son, who had died in a plane crash at the age of thirty-three just ten years before? He had also loved the lake with a passion. Could he be waiting? Watching over his little brother?

To logical Western minds, these are wild imaginings, only fit for fanciful dreams on lonely nights when the subconscious ranges into unknown territory. But what if the Balinese mystics are correct? What if the soul of the departed is indeed reborn into another living body? What if the spirits of those we love are allowed one last visit to the places and persons who have been most dear to them?

If this is so, then I believe my prayers have been answered. My son's spirit has found a home. I remember another passage in his journal:

> *I wonder if it is not my purpose…the reason the Gods have brought me to Bali…to simply live with the animals…I hope it will be in this life, but I am content if it is in the next.*